Walking the Scottish Borders
and East Lothian

Clan Walk Guides

Walking the Scottish Borders and East Lothian

Walking Scotland Series
Volume 19

Mary Welsh
and
Christine Isherwood

First published by Clan Books, 2011

ISBN 978 1873597 35 4
Text and Illustrations
© Mary Welsh
and Christine Isherwood 2011

The authors wish to express their gratitude to
Edward Welsh, Tom Welsh, Jennifer Outhwaite and Mike Isherwood
for their help in preparing this volume

Clan Books
Clandon House
The Cross, Doune
Perthshire
FK16 6BE

Printed and bound in Great Britain by
Bell & Bain Ltd., Glasgow

Publisher's Note

In this new volume, 'Walking the Scottish Borders and East Lothian', our authors have set out to tempt you to share their love of a delectable and perhaps under-valued treasure-chest. They have gleaned a rich harvest of walks that celebrate the immense variety of locations that the area has to offer. These include a wealth of delightful villages, reached down leafy lanes, from where it is just an easy walk to the banks of the many rivers and burns. There are rambles through deciduous and coniferous forests, which adorn the very steepest of slopes, good walks for those days when there is a need for shelter from both wind and rain. They have described ascents over high rounded hills, where splendid grassy tracks encourage walkers to explore the heights. Some of these range far from the nearest habitation. As always, such expeditions need to be prudently timed, and it is essential to take reliable clothing and equipment, plus reserve rations in case of unplanned delays. More walks visit the many sites of unrivalled prehistoric and historic interest just waiting to be explored.

It is a wonderful area, which keeps its lovely secrets tucked away; secrets that are often by-passed by those hurrying towards the Highlands and Islands.

The Authors' Golden Rules
for Good, Safe Walking

- Wear suitable clothes and take adequate waterproofs.
- Walk in strong footwear; walking boots are advisable.
- Carry the relevant map and a compass and know how to use them.
- Carry a whistle; remember six long blasts repeated at one minute intervals is the distress signal.
- Do not walk alone, and tell someone where you are going.
- If mist descends, return.
- Keep all dogs under strict control. Observe all "No Dogs" notices – they are there for very good reasons.

In all volumes of the WALKING SCOTLAND series, the authors make every effort to ensure accuracy, but changes can occur after publication. Reports of such changes are welcomed by the publisher. Neither the publisher nor the authors can accept responsibility for errors, omissions or any loss or injury.

Contents

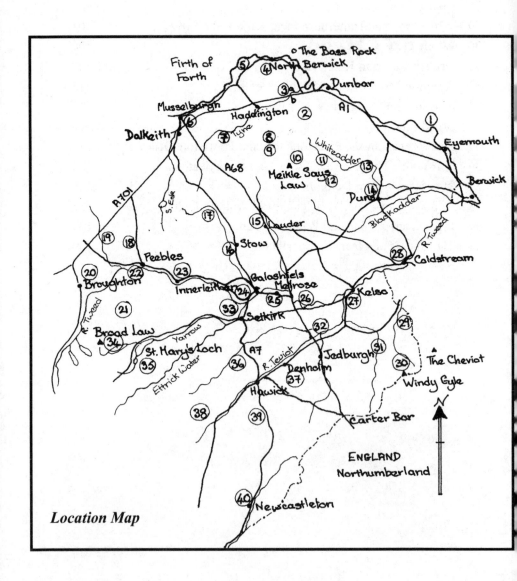

The Bass Rock

Firth of Forth

⑤ ④ North Berwick

Dunbar

③a b

A1

Musselburgh

Haddington ②

Dalkeith ⑥

⑦ Tyne ⑧

⑨

A68

⑩

Meikle Says Law

Whiteadder

⑪

⑬

⑫

Duns ⑭

Blackadder

R. Tweed

Eyemouth

Berwick

R.701

S. Esk

⑰

⑮ Lauder

⑲

⑱

⑯ Stow

Peebles

⑳ Broughton

㉒

㉓

Innerleithen ㉔

Galashiels

Melrose

⑳㉖

㉘ Coldstream

Kelso ㉗

R. Tweed

㉑

⑳㉕

㉓㉕ Selkirk

㉒

Broad Law

㉞ St. Mary's Loch

Yarrow

A7

㉜

㉛ ㉙

Jedburgh

㉚

㉟

Ettrick Water

㊱

R. Teviot

Denholm

㊲

The Cheviot

Windy Gyle

Hawick

N

㊳

㊴

Carter Bar

ENGLAND
Northumberland

㊵ Newcastleton

Location Map

St Abb's Head

Park in the tiny village of St Abb's, grid ref 918673. There is very little space so best get there early. To park overlooking the shore there is a fee required.

This walk starts from the fishing village of St Abb's, taking its name from **St Aebba** who was shipwrecked, around AD 640, on a nearby headland. Eventually he was made head of a nearby monastic settlement. This was destroyed at the end of the 9th century by the Vikings or the Scots.

The delightful **Mire Loch** is a long narrow freshwater loch. It snuggles between grassy hills, their slopes partly lined with decidu-ous trees and gorse, the latter when in bloom perfumes the air. There are paths on either side and these, in spring, are lined with great clumps of primroses. Towards the head of the loch are vast areas of reeds. Yellowhammer, willow warbler and chiffchaff call from the numerous nesting sites.

St Abb's Head lighthouse was commissioned in 1872. Just beyond the lighthouse keepers' cottages, look back to see the great globe of the light, not on a

Pettico Wick, St Abb's Head

tall stack but a square platform on the sloping cliffs. Lower down stands the foghorn, large and bright red.

1 Climb up from the parking area by a long stairway of wooden steps that start to the left of the café to reach a delightful viewpoint, with a fascinating memorial to 'The Disaster', when in 1881 a great storm struck the east coast of Scotland and many men were lost at sea, leaving women widowed and children fatherless. From the viewpoint there is a fine view over the harbour and along the coast to Coldingham. Walk on up the B6438 and, a short way along, on the left side of the road, continue on the signed footpath with the wall to your right, keeping you safe from the traffic. At its end, cross the road and walk on along a similar footpath. Go on ahead at the end of the

path and keep to the left of the National Nature Reserve Visitor Centre, which you might wish to visit. Pass through the car park, to join a narrow road and turn right. This is the road to the lighthouse.

2 Walk on. Ignore a left turn to a house and just beyond take to a grassy swathe, just left of the road and continue until it rejoins the road. Then follow the road as it winds right, crosses a cattle grid and climbs. Where it begins to bear left at a corner, leave the road to take a gated track descending right, with sheep pasture to the left and deciduous trees beyond the wall to your right. Soon you can see Mire Loch, blue and sparkling through the trees. Just beyond the National Nature Reserve notice board, where the track winds right, leave it along a narrow path, with the loch below to your right, Carry on this lovely

path, between great banks of gorse, where violets and primroses grow in profusion in the spring. At the end of the loch, a narrow path continues on to rejoin the lighthouse road.

Guillemots

3 Pause here for a magnificent view of Pettico Wick, a long stretch of jagged rocks around which the sea boils, overshadowed by awesome cliffs. Walk right along the road, past a small parking area and follow the road round right, with a fine view down to Mire Loch. Look for sea pink flowering here. The road then comes close to the several huge sea inlets where almost sheer-sided cliffs descend to the turquoise water below. Here move left, off the road, and pause to see, in spring and summer, thousands of seabirds nesting on the narrow ledges. Look for fulmars, kittiwakes, razorbills, guillemots, shags and maybe puffins staking out their tiny space for their nests and to tend their young. Then rejoin the road and follow it up to the lighthouse. There is no public access.

4 Bear slightly right of the gate and climb up a narrow path to walk above the lighthouse keepers' houses and then look back to see the huge light and the foghorn. Carry on along the obvious path over Kirk Hill and then descend to a junction of paths. Here take the wide grassy swathe, keeping right of some very high cliffs. Go through a gate and pass two delightful bays, below to the left. Then begin a steepish climb up a stepped way. Pause half way to look right to see Mire Loch once more. Continue on up the side of Bell Hill and at the brow pause to enjoy the splendid view of St Abb's harbour and the coast beyond. Take care because as the way begins to descend it comes close to the cliff edge.

5 Stroll on to pass a dramatic row of jagged rocks high above the sea. And then go on descending above Starney Bay, past a seat and then bear left above the bay. Pause at the picnic table to look across to the

gull-whitened cliffs and the high-level jagged rocks once more. Turn right, away from the sea and walk a track, beside a high wall on the left. Continue to the road. Cross and join the protected footpath, taken at the outset of your walk, and descend to the harbour and your vehicle.

Thrift

Walk 2

Pressmennan Wood

Park just inside Pressmennan Wood at a small parking area, grid ref 622725. Access this from the centre of the village of Stenton by a narrow road, south. Drive through Ruchlaw West Mains farm and continue steeply uphill for a short way, then left along a rough track at a sign for the wood.

The village of **Stenton** goes back to the 1500s. Both then, and now, it is an agricultural village, with large fields and sheep pastures.

The Tron, Stenton

The photogenic reconstructed tron or weighbeam on East Green are reminders of how important the wool trade was.

The Forestry Commission first planted the 220 acres of Pressmennan Wood. Now it is owned by **The Woodland Trust** and the public are welcome to walk its tracks and paths and along part of the lake.

Walk 2

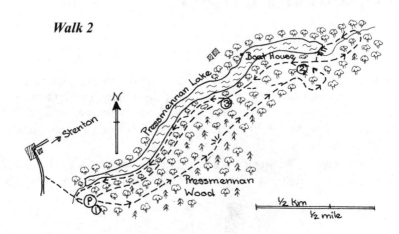

1 Take the higher of two tracks that lead from the parking area. Beyond the gate, go on steadily ascending through the mature woodland, where you might spot roe deer. Soon the trees thin out and you reach a viewpoint and a seat. Pause here and enjoy a distant sighting of Bass Rock and North Berwick Law. Continue on the path, narrower now and almost level. Follow it until you can take a wide curve that brings you down on a mainly stepped way to the main track.

2 Carry on right along the track and go with it as it curves left, ignoring two wooden gates into open pasture, through which runs tree-lined Bennet's Burn, the overflow of Pressmennan Lake. Wind on round, left, on the good track through the pleasing woodland, where you might flush a woodcock. Cross the dam, pausing again to enjoy the view up the long snake-shaped lake. Go up steps, followed by a path to join the main track once more. Stride right, descend a slope and carry on until you reach a 'sculptured' waymarker – a wooden block with a hole in it.

3 Turn right down two steps and then drop steadily towards the lake. Follow the path as it runs along the lakeshore, descending a little to

pass through rhododendrons, just above the water. Look for mallards and in winter many goldeneye. Soon you reach a fallen tree across the path, with steps and a handrail to help you across. Where the lake ends here, in a marsh, curve round left and walk up beside a stream with wild garlic on its banks and in late winter carpets of snowdrops higher up. Come out on to a track and turn left, then immediately left again and up a path to arrive at the car park.

Woodcock

Practicals

Type of walk: *A quiet walk through fine mixed woodland, with a pleasing return along the side of the lake.*

Total distance: 3½ miles/5.5km
Time: 1½–2 hours
Maps: OS Explorer 351/Landranger 67

Walk 3a

East Linton and Preston Mill

Park in the square at East Linton, grid ref 592773, or in the plentiful off-road parking. Access the village from the A199 off the A1.

The 16th century stone **Preston Mill** is set in idyllic countryside. With its conical- shaped roof, red pantiles and oast-house shape it is a great inspiration for photographers. Close by is the Doocot (dovecote), which provided winter shelter for pigeons and food for their owners.

The **16th century bridge** over the River Tyne was crossed, in 1603, by James VI of Scotland on his way to England to become James I of Great Britain. It is still in use today. Under it flows the petulant river, the linn, which gives its name to the village.

Preston Mill

1 Set off from the square, north, downhill along the main street until you can turn right into Preston Road. Go past the fine Kirk, on the left, and, just beyond, cross the road and take the signposted path that  leads down to the river. Bear left on a grassy trod, passing a weir that controls water to a leat. Cross a footbridge over the leat, now on your left, to reach Preston Mill, where you will want to have your camera handy.

Walk 3A

2 Turn right on another grassy trod and slant across the pasture to a white footbridge over the River Tyne. Once across turn left to walk a fine track along the side of the river. Wind round right with the river beside you and carry on. At the next bridge, turn away from it and walk the unsigned track beside the huge pasture. Look in the pool on the left where you may see a heron. At the T-junction walk right to view the Phantassie Doocot.

3 Continue on along the track to reach the weir and return by your outward route.

Heron

Practicals

Type of walk: *A short walk, full of interest on mainly good tracks and paths.*

Total distance: 1½ miles/2.4km

Time: 1 hour

Maps: Explorer 351, Landranger 67

Walk 3b

East Linton, Traprain Law and Hailes Castle

Park in the square at East Linton or any available space along the main street, grid ref 592773. Access this from the A199 off the A1.

Traprain Law was a commanding position for prehistoric communities who could demonstrate their control of the surrounding area. Many artifacts found revealed occupation during the Bronze Age and by around 1500 BC the Votadini were using the Law as a burial site. Much of the hill is covered with unimproved grassland, with a few patches of gorse and elder. Where the soil is thinner look for tormentil, primrose and meadow saxifrage. Skylarks and meadow pipits serenade you as you climb.

An information board at **Hailes Castle** describes its turbulent history. It was owned by the Hepburns, one of whom was Mary Queen of Scots' third

Hailes Castle

husband. The castle controlled trade through the valley and the family grew rich from the tolls. The ruin is picturesque and set in glorious countryside. It has two pit dungeons which will intrigue youngsters.

1 Descend south from where you have parked and wind round left on the B1377. Cross the 16th century bridge over the River Tyne. Walk a short way on the pavement then cross the road to pass under the railway bridge. Beyond, go on along Lauder Place, following signs for Hailes and Haddington. Climb steadily uphill and at the A199, cross with care, and follow the sign for Hailes Castle. Once the houses are left behind, continue on the almost traffic-free narrow road, Brae Heads, high above the superb Tyne Valley, with fine views of Traprain Law.

2 Soon the lane passes under the huge viaduct, carrying the A1 Expressway, which is strung across this lovely valley. Carry on along the lane, Brae Heads Loan, to take the first left turn, a steep tarmacked road, which brings you to attractive Kippielaw farmhouse. Pause here

Walk 3b

½ Km

½ mile

to get your breath back, then take the continuing track to the right of the attractive dwellings. Wind round with the track, which can be muddy after it has been used by horse riders. At the end, turn right along the B-road below Traprain Law to reach the picnic area where there are some interesting information boards.

17

3 Climb the stile and walk ahead on the level path, which soon begins to climb keeping high and parallel above the wall below on the right. Follow it as it climbs again and curves round left. It then ascends steadily to a waymark, which directs you ahead to the white painted trig point (729ft/221m) and stone shelter. The views are superb. If there is a north wind blowing, walk on a short way to have your picnic in the shelter of some rocks and enjoy an even more dramatic view into the valley of the Luggate Burn.

4 Return to the trig point and descend by the same route until you reach the start of the level area above the wall. Here take a narrower, easy-to-miss path, off left, and leading to the side of the wall. The distinct path takes you, west, through a gap between the wall and a hedge of gorse bushes to a stile, over the wall, a short way along. Bear left along the road, for a ¼ mile/0.5km, then turn right into a signed track and go with it where it turns right to pass between hedgerows. After ¼mile/0.5km it winds left and then right and continues beside a wall on the right.

5 The track curves left down a rather wet way through pleasing deciduous woodland and leads to a narrow lane. Bear left to reach Hailes

Meadow Saxifrage

Castle, which is well worth a visit and will please any youngsters on the walk. After your explorations return along the road to take the signposted right of way, left, that leads to a very long footbridge over the River Tyne and across several islands where the river has braided. At the far side, walk right along a path signed for East Linton. This is a delightful riverside way, where you might spot dippers bobbing up and down on rocks. After 1½ miles/2.5km the path takes you under the Expressway viaduct again.

Dipper

Eventually the path climbs steps and winds on high above the river on a railed way. At the end of the track, turn left up a road to cross the B1407 just before the railway bridge on your right. Pass under the bridge and curve left uphill on Bridge Street to return to where you have parked.

Snowdrops and primroses

Practicals

Type of walk: *A very pleasing walk along paths, tracks and quiet roads.*

Total distance: 6½ miles/10.5km

Time: 3–4 hours

Maps: OS Explorer 351/Landranger 67

Walk 4

North Berwick Law and town walk

Park in the car park in the centre of North Berwick, grid ref 555853.

The word Law is an old Scots word for a rounded, conical hill. **North Berwick Law**, 613ft/187m, is all that is left of a plug of lava that once welled up within an active volcano at this site. Everything else was eroded away by the movement of ice during the ice age, leaving just a cone of harder material, which was once deep underground.

The attractive town of North Berwick, set against the impressive back drop of North Berwick Law, stands on the splendid East Lothian coast. It has sweeping sandy beaches, sheltered coves and several islands. As a fishing and trading port it dates back to the 14th century. It is probably best known for its superb **Bass Rock**, just offshore, with its seemingly diminutive lighthouse and its enormous colony of breeding gannets. It is another volcanic plug and marks the point where the Firth of Forth joins the North Sea.

*Doocot and
North Berwick Law*

Historically, the **Law was used as a watchtower** to warn of the coming of would-be invaders entering the Firth. The watch was at one time a duty of nuns in the nearby Cistercian convent, and the car park information board carries a dramatic picture of a nun, dressed in her habit, lighting the warning fire when Henry VIII's ships appeared in 1544. A little below the summit are the remains of a stone building used during the Napoleonic Wars to watch out for French ships. Nearby are the ruins of a brick and concrete structure used as a lookout post in World War II. Also on the summit is the huge replica of a pair of whale's jawbones. Real jawbones were first erected in 1709 and became a familiar feature of the town's skyline. The first set blew down in a gale in 1935 and were replaced, and the current pair, made of fibreglass, were erected in 2008.

1 Leave the parking area in the direction of the town centre. Turn left into Quality Street. Cross and walk past the Tourist Information Centre. Cross the road by the small roundabout and follow the John Muir Way (JMW) sign, which directs you through an arch in the middle of a fine white building, the entrance to Lodge Gardens. Beyond the arch, wind right and uphill, then cross a wide grass, tree-lined space to an information board at the far side. Walk straight ahead up Lady Jane Road. Ignore the sign for the Law. Cross St Baldred's Road. Where Lady Jane Road turns left, bear right on a footpath through trees. Cross Coupar Avenue and Gilbert Avenue and walk down a grassy space between houses to Lochbridge Road. Turn right and walk out to the end to turn left just before the main road (Law Road) and follow the footpath to the end to reach the car park below the Law.

Walk 4

2 Read the interesting information boards before you set off up the Law and then go through the gate/ stile to follow a wide stony path, which leads first southwards and then eastwards up

21

the southern side, with gorse on the left and pleasant mixed woodland on the right. Soon a narrower path, signposted to the summit, leads off left. Now on the western side of the hill, the path swings northwards and becomes a broad grassy path as it climbs, revealing splendid views across the Firth of Forth and to the Pentland Hills, as well as looking down on North Berwick with its harbour.

3 Then the path becomes steeper and more rocky and, as you near the summit, there is no clearly defined path and walkers will have to find their own way between outcrops. Some easy scrambling may be necessary. At the top a view indicator helps walkers identify the many points of interest, including, as well as the Pentlands, the Ochils, the Lomond Hills, Largo Law in Fife, the Isle of May, the Bass Rock, Traprain Law, the Lammermuirs, and Edinburgh's Arthur's Seat.

4 Return from the summit by the same route. Turn left on the main track, still the JMW. At the next junction, leave the way and turn left to wind round the base of the Law. At the next Y-junction follow the left branch, a lovely grassy track below cliffs. Join the path coming in on the right and climb a little to a narrower way contouring the hillside on the east. Eventually this winds right and runs along a ridge, with a spectacular view of the Bass rock. Go through a gap by a gate and on along a track to reach some houses. The cylindrical tower in the field to your right is a doocot (see walk 3a). Go down right between the houses to a road.

5 Turn left; at the next corner the pavement ends, so cross and walk, with care, down the right side to a roundabout. Cross the main road to the right and take the path on the far side which winds right among trees. Almost immediately walk left down to cross a bridge and turn right into The Glen. Enjoy the path as it follows the burn down through deciduous trees with ferns and winter heliotrope and accompanied by woodland bird song. On the way you pass ruins of various mills. Take the right branch at the bottom by a picnic area and go on down to the shore road.

6 Turn left along the sandy beach, where you might spot gannets winging their way to the Bass Rock. Listen for the

Winter Heliotrope

22

delightful cooing of eiders as you go. Come up onto the road again at the end, beyond the open-air swimming pool. Turn right to see the ruins of St Andrew's Chapel, the Scottish Seabird Centre and the attractive harbour. Go down steps to the harbour and then through a gate to walk left along Victoria Road. Cross Melbourne Place and continue along Quality Street to turn left into the car park.

Gannets

Practicals

Type of walk: *Pleasant town walk, well signed on good paths, through parkland and up a notable landmark. A stretch along the beach near the end of the walk. Lots of interest along the way.*

Total distance: 3 miles/5km

Time: 2–3 hours

Map: OS Explorer 351/Landranger 66 and 67

Walk 5

Dirleton and Gullane

Park at the huge Yellow Craig car park, grid ref 515855, close to a vast shelterbelt of Scots pines. This is accessed from North Berwick by the A198 and then by a right turn a short way along the B1345, at the east end of Dirleton.

Sea Buckthorn was planted in the 1970s to help stabilise some of the sand dunes and protect them from damage. Unfortunately the plant took over and has now become a pest. It covers vast areas, invading the dunes and making some paths difficult to walk. There is an on-going programme to rid the area of the pest but there is so much to do to remove it that this may never be achieved. It does provide nest sites for birds and protection for foxes and roe deer but its thorns are very sharp and bare legs will suffer. In winter fieldfares live on the glorious orange berries.

Sea Buckthorn

Gullane is a pleasing village with many fine large houses and you may wish to make a diversion on your walk to visit it. When the railway came in 1898 it turned the village into a resort and a golfing mecca.

1   From the parking area turn left, pass through more pines, cross the John Muir Way (JMW) and go ahead through shallow sand dunes to the seashore. Look ahead to see Fidra Island, with its fine lighthouse and masses of sea birds on the rocky lump. Walk left along a sandy path at the top of the beach, with marram grass to the left, then a tangle of sea buckthorn behind which stand more stately pines. When you reach a large boulder field, take a small path through the marram for a more comfortable walk.

2   Continue on over more sand to reach another boulder field of rough rocks. Here look for a sandy path leading into the buckthorn, giving

a fine sheltered walk. Carry on along the path parallel with a wire fence, which surrounds Marine Villa and another house. Then when the buckthorn becomes too rampant, look for an ancient outflow pipe down on the sands and

Eiders

descend to the beach and carry on along large plates of easy-to-walk rock. The path above does continue but the buckthorn has made it very unpleasant to walk through – unless you have some secateurs. Further along the rocky slabs you can see lots of escape routes back up to the path if the tide takes you unaware. As you go enjoy the cooing of dozens of eiders out at sea.

3 Pass under huge 'bulges' of rock, rather like mountain buttresses, named 'Hanging Rocks' on the map. Then the buckthorn ceases and marram grass covers shallow dunes. Here look for a tiny cairn at the top of the beach marking the start of a path through the dunes. Look

Walk 5

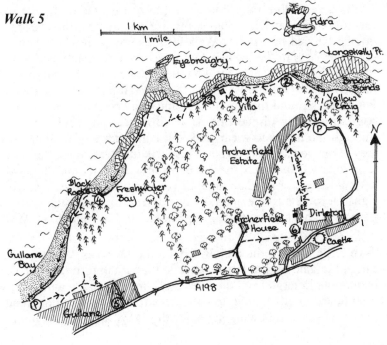

The Bass Rock, Craigleith and the Lamb from Longskelly

across to see Eyebroughy island then follow the grassy track and wind round right, ignoring all other turns. Wind round again on a wide track and curve left with high dunes to the left and more shallow ones to the right, following a clear vehicle track. Just before the path drops down to the shore, turn left to walk a narrow path just above it. Enjoy the view over to the Fife coast. Then you reach an area of black boulders and here use a good path just above the shoreline and walk round Freshwater Haven.

4 At the far end climb the slope to a grassy area. Go on by the scanty remains of St Patrick's chapel, picturesque against the ever-present orange-berried buckthorn. Walk on the good path where you might see stonechats in the bushes. Out to sea look for gannets diving and innumerable eiders. Pass through the dunes close to the shore to reach the enormous Gullane Bay with the huge Hummell rocks at Gullane Point. Walk round the bay on the sand to come to a post with a white bag that holds a rescue line. Here turn left and climb up the path through the dunes to a car park. Pleasing views of Gullane village may tempt you to make a visit. This walk turns left along the edge of a level grassy field, where there is a row of seats. Continue on in front of several bungalows and go on until you can pass through a gate on the right. Beyond, strike diagonally over a field to the far top corner and pass through a kissing gate, giving access to Muirfield road. Walk on up to join the busy A198.

5 Turn left and walk the metalled path, the JMW for ½ mile/1km. Go through a gate on the left to walk a wide track through Half Moon plantation. Emerge from the trees and continue on a good track, with crop fields on either side, to come to a road. Cross and descend left for a few steps, following signs for the JMW and then turn up right

along a narrow lane, its tarmac hidden by an impacted layer of soil. Soon the tarmac is revealed and the pleasant gorse-lined way goes on. Follow it until you reach the very large, charming green at the village of Dirleton. Attractive houses border most of the green but the north side is taken up by Dirleton Castle, almost obscured by large trees. Perhaps you will have time for a seat on the green to enjoy the ambience. If you wish to visit the castle there is a charge for entry.

6 From the green, walk down a side road towards the church, with its unusual tower. Continue, keeping to the right side of it, to join a well signed track, more of the JMW, for ¾ mile/1.4km, with vast crop fields on either side from where come, in spring, the calls of green and golden plover and curlews. On reaching a long strip of Scots pine, follow the track as it bears right. A short way along the track enters the pines and goes on ahead to the car park.

Golden Plover

Practicals

Type of walk: *Very pleasant along a delightful stretch of the coast with sandy tracks, grassy tracks and with some rocks to clamber over. Some unavoidable road walking and then the JMW brings you back to the car park.*

Total distance: 8–9 miles/13–14.5km.

Time: 4–5 hours

Maps: OS Explorer 351/Landranger 66

Walk 6

Musselburgh

Park in the signed free car park beside the River Esk, Musselburgh, grid ref 345728. Access this by turning north off the main street, about half way along.

Inveresk village, with its fine villas and mansions, stands on the crest of a hill, laid out overlooking a bow of the River Esk. The strategic position now occupied by the church of St Michael, on its hill, attracted the attention of the Votadini tribe and of the Romans. Here the Duke of Somerset created a mound on which to stand his cannon in 1547. The former church was witness to an army of 30,000 Scots and when defeated by the English they lost 10,000 soldiers. Cromwell was also drawn to this site and he stabled his horses in the church.

The River Esk carries rich silt, which is deposited at the river mouth, giving rise to extensive mudflats at low tide. Between tides this area is teeming with shellfish, worms and other creatures, which attract innumerable waders, gulls and swans. The land on which you stand used

Old Bridge, Musselburgh

28

to be covered twice daily by the tide. The seawall was built to accommodate waste ash from Cockenzie Power Station.

1 Cross the footbridge at the back of the car park and walk upstream to pass bridges across the river, including under a very low one; walkers over 5ft 2ins must bend low. Carry on enjoying the colourful beds of flowers, and the ducks, geese and gulls on the water, to cross over a busy road, with care, and then take a slip path down to cross another footbridge over the surging river and walk right. Stroll on along a narrow road past factory premises and then make use of a little path that comes close to the water again where all the bustle and busyness is left behind. Follow the now tarmacked track as it continues close to the Esk, which is edged with fine trees and bushes. Go past a dramatic weir and carry on.

Firth of Forth

John Muir Way

Ash Lagoons

Reserve

Levenhall Links

Racecourse

A6095
½ km
½ mile

Musselburgh

N

Walk 6

Eskmills

Inveresk

Weir

River Esk

2 Then the track moves out into open country, with a golf course on the opposite bank. Here you may wish to take a little path through trees and bushes on the edge of the water, to the right of the trackway. Pass under a sturdy stone bridge and a metal bridge, both of which carry the railway. Dawdle on into the countryside, ignoring a wide bridge on the right. As you go on, look for where there was once a ford across

29

the Esk and, a few steps beyond, look for a signpost, on the left, almost obscured by trees. This directs you uphill on steps through a small wood and then on ahead beside a large arable field.

3 At the next signpost, walk left along a wide grassy track that passes between two huge fields. Keep on in the same direction to reach the road through Inveresk. Turn left and walk along ignoring the right turn taken by the main road until you reach the 16th century church of St Michael, which you might like to visit. Then take a ginnel opposite the church and after a short descent walk the upper path through many fine trees, high above the river. Go past two seats and then descend steps, left, to the side of the river once more. Turn right and continue on your outward route, where you might spot goldeneye and kingfisher. Go past the weir and stroll on to the car park. Once here you might wish to extend your walk in the opposite direction.

4 From the parking area, stroll on with the lovely Esk to your left and the houses of Goosegreen to the right, along the John Muir Way. Continue on until you

Kingfisher

can see where the river exits from the land to join the sea. Pause here to see the Fife coast and the Lomond Hills. Look left to see Arthur's seat just on the edge of Edinburgh. If the tide is low and you have your binoculars, spend some time looking at the birds. You might spot long-tailed duck and common scoter, goldeneye and eiders.

Long-tailed Duck and Common Scoters

5 At the next information board, turn right and walk away from the sea. Look for twites and reed buntings on the fence or atop bushes, edging the very pleasing path, soon to wind round a large lagoon. Pause again here. Where you now stand would have been under the water; it was reclaimed in the 1960s by Scottish Power. As the lagoons have filled they have been pleasingly landscaped.

6 At the next information board, turn right along the fine path, which eventually continues below a huge heap of power station waste. Then you reach a T-junction and turn left along a muddy wide track where the wagons carrying the waste have churned up the track. Then bear right and choose the driest way with, away to your left, Musselburgh racecourse, the oldest in Scotland. Carry on ahead to rejoin your outward path and turn left to return to the car park.

Red Bunting

Practicals

Type of walk: *An interesting walk with an unusual extension.*

Total distance: 7 miles/11.3km

Time: 3–4 hours

Maps: OS Explorer 351/ Landranger 66

Walk 7

Pencaitland

Off street parking 200yds/200m along Lempockwells Road, grid ref 443687, almost opposite the turning to the railway track walk, Huntlaw Road.

East Lothian's River Tyne divides the village into **East Pencaitland and Wester Pencaitland** and the stone bridge that was built in 1510 to connect two parts of the village still stands today. It is crossed by modern traffic in a single direction at a time and is controlled by traffic lights. Close to the bridge and on the east side of the river is the parish church. It has an unusual and attractive tower, which served as a belfry and maybe a dovecot.

A **mercat cross** is a market cross and was found where trade and commerce was part of the economic life of a Scottish city, town, and village. It was where merchants would gather, executions take place, and where proclamations and announcements were made.

Gifford and Garvald light railway track has been replaced by an easy-to-walk, well-surfaced footpath. The railway was closed in 1965 by Dr Beeching. At its peak about 30,000 passengers used the line.

1 Walk up Huntlaw Road and just before the railway bridge, climb the steps, left, onto the railway track. Turn left and walk the good track to pass the first of several plaques that give

Doocot, Saltoun

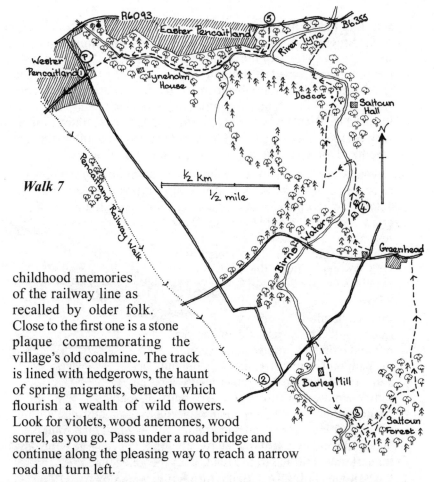

Walk 7

childhood memories
of the railway line as
recalled by older folk.
Close to the first one is a stone
plaque commemorating the
village's old coalmine. The track
is lined with hedgerows, the haunt
of spring migrants, beneath which
flourish a wealth of wild flowers.
Look for violets, wood anemones, wood
sorrel, as you go. Pass under a road bridge and
continue along the pleasing way to reach a narrow
road and turn left.

2 Stroll on the almost traffic-free road, past a garden with geese and
ducks cavorting on a pond and a stream. Go on to cross a fine bridge
over Birns Water and, just beyond, turn right along a track signed to
Barley Mill, once an 18th century pearl barley mill. As you approach
the gate to the mill, go through a gap, on the left, through a wall and a
fence, and turn right to walk a wide grassy swathe to pass the delightful buildings in this very attractive corner. Go through the gate at the
end and follow a green trod that keeps parallel with the fenced woodland to the left.

3 Wind round left with the fence to enter Saltoun Wood. The path climbs
up through fine trees, with glimpses to your right of the river below.
Continue gently upwards passing through wood anemone and wood

33

sorrel, in the spring, and wood rush carpeting all the woodland floor. At the brow take a narrow path going off left soon to join a wider path, where you turn left to wind on through more splendid trees, with sheep pasture away to the left. Remain on this until it eventually becomes reinforced and bends left to a road. Turn left and descend to an unclassified road on the right. Just before the house on the corner, walk up the road to a gate on your left. Beyond the gate is a stretch of fencing with useful stones on either side. Step over here and follow the fenced woodland, on your left, all the way round, right, to a gate.

4   Beyond, follow a narrow path that leads into more woodland, with the river down below to the left. Enjoy the path as it widens and passes below fine beech and limes. At a T-junction turn left and cross a footbridge over the river. Walk ahead along a fenced green swathe to a metal gate. Pause here and look right to see the turreted Saltoun Hall towering over the parkland. Go through the gate, climb up the slope and turn right along a grassy track, with sheep pasture to the left and woodland to the right. Soon the path moves into deciduous woodland

Willow warbler

and curves left to pass a rather lonely-looking folly once used as a doocot. Carry on to a small triangle of grass and drop down right to cross a footbridge unsafe for vehicles. Turn left beyond and a short way beyond, turn right below a huge redwood tree, leaving the river behind. Pass a large bungalow on the left and continue to the road, with the gatehouse to the Saltoun Hall to your right. Turn left to walk down the road, facing the oncoming traffic.

5   After a quarter of a mile, you reach a large white bungalow to your right. Cross here to a large layby, where there is a bus stop, and go through a barrier to walk a continuing signposted track. A short way along, before you reach the gates to the sewage works, descend a slope, unsigned, down to the side of the river and walk, right, along a pleasing path. Where there is a choice of paths at a split

Wood Sorrel

always take the one beside the river. Stroll on the lovely way along a good path, with the river chuckling away to your left and a wide area of trees to your right, until your reach a metal bridge, which you cross. Go on along a path, which soon winds right. On reaching the parking area for the Care Home, turn right and then left to reach your vehicle, perhaps with time left to walk down the road, right, to view the Mercat Cross in the middle of a little green area.

Mallards

Practicals

Type of walk: *A delightful, mainly level walk of contrasts, railway track, woodland, riverside, and parkland.*

Total distance: 6½ miles /10.5km

Time: 3–4 hours

Maps: OS Explorer 345/Landranger 66

Walk 8

Gifford to Bolton

Park in the square of the village of Gifford, grid ref 534681. Access this by A6369 from Haddington.

   The **picturesque village of Gifford** lies 4 miles/6.5km south of Haddington on the Gifford Water. It dates from the late 17th century and was originally built to replace the village of Bothans, which was demolished to make way for the walled park around Yester House. It was built to house estate workers.

   Bolton church dates from 1806 on the site of two earlier churches. The mother, brother and sister of Robert Burns are buried in the churchyard.

1 Walk up through the village towards the fine church and wind on round, on the pavement, left, to walk out of the village for less than ½ mile/0.6km, using the grassy verge. Once over the Sandyford Burn, descend the signposted steps to walk on through the trees about the stream, with fields to the right. A short way along bear right by the side of the winding Colstoun Water. Go through a kissing gate that cuts off a bend in the burn and walk on past white butterbur growing along its banks. Look for dippers as you go and long tailed tits in the hedge. Follow the signpost in the direction of Bolton and pass through a gate into mixed woodland.

Doocot, Bolton

2 Emerge from the trees and pass through a gateless gap

36

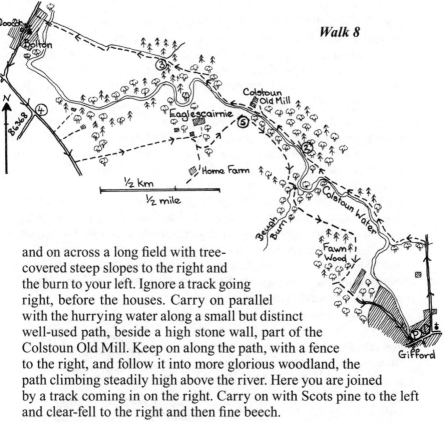

and on across a long field with tree-
covered steep slopes to the right and
the burn to your left. Ignore a track going
right, before the houses. Carry on parallel
with the hurrying water along a small but distinct
well-used path, beside a high stone wall, part of the
Colstoun Old Mill. Keep on along the path, with a fence
to the right, and follow it into more glorious woodland, the
path climbing steadily high above the river. Here you are joined
by a track coming in on the right. Carry on with Scots pine to the left
and clear-fell to the right and then fine beech.

3 Go over the stile to the right of a gate and walk the path between vast
fields. Follow the tractor-marked path as it winds a little left and then
right and continues as a very good path, with a hedge to your right.
Ahead you have a fine view of Bolton church surrounded by trees.
Cross the Colstoun Water by a bridge and walk up the slope to a road
and turn left to pass through the village of Bolton. To your left is the
church and in its churchyard are buried the relatives of Robert Burns.
Opposite is an interesting Doocot, part of a farm steading and now
being developed for housing. After a few steps the tiny hamlet ends
and this walk continues on along the pavement beside the road. When
the pavement runs out, cross the road to walk the wide grassy verge.
Follow the way round a large bend and then climb, using the verge, for
½ mile/1km.

4 At the top of the hill where the road swings away right, go ahead on the
lesser road and stroll on to take the third left turn, unsigned. Stroll this
traffic-free, tarmacked avenue, lined with lofty beech and other forest

trees for ½ mile/1km. Just after passing a fine house, Eaglescairnie, wind right and almost immediately take a path on the left (the waymark, a red ring on a wooden post, is tucked out of immediate sight). Walk ahead, over a humpy narrow ridge and pass through a gateless gap in the fence. Head over a large pasture to the far right corner where there is a signposted kissing gate.

5 Beyond, walk the fine grassy path beside a large field on the right, with a good view of the Lammermuir Hills beyond, and a tall beech hedge to the left. Behind the hedge is a long strip of forest trees and far below the Colstoun Water, where you walked earlier. Head on to a signpost directing you left for Gifford. Descend a muddy path to cross a footbridge over the Beugh Burn, a tributary of Colstoun Water. Walk on through deciduous woodland to follow a narrow path up a slope to pass through a signposted gate. Go ahead beside the hedge on you right to an amusing two-armed signpost which says 'Back Again' and 'There". Follow 'Back Again' to walk beside Fawn Wood and curve round the corner, with the trees still to your right and follow the path through scrub vegetation to take, left, a wide signposted track through decidu-ous vegetation. Continue ahead when you reach several houses and where the track becomes tarmacked. This road goes on to cross the Colstoun Water and then leads up to the square at Gifford, beside where you have parked.

Long-tailed Tit

Practicals

Type of walk: *Very interesting and enjoyable. There is about a mile of road walking, but there are easy verges all the way and little traffic. The remainder of the walk is a delight.*

Total distance: 5½ miles/9km
Time: 2–3 hours
Maps: OS Explorer 351/Landranger 66

Walk 9

Hopes Reservoir

Park just before the Water Board buildings, grid ref 558633. To access this, drive down the main street of the village of Gifford and continue ahead for a short distance to a three-way junction. Turn sharp left, along an unclassified road, to Longyester farm and turn left through the farm buildings. Immediately turn right along a narrow lane. Park on the right beside the fence, just before the waterboard buildings, taking care not to block access to it or the farmer's gate.

Hopes Reservoir was constructed in the 1930s to provide water for towns in the area. It is a very shapely pool, with fine deciduous trees and bushes around its shores. In spring a host of willow warblers give their melodious calls from many of the trees. Grouse call from the heather on the higher hills, the slopes of which are a glorious purple in summer.

1 Walk on from where you have parked to pass to the right of the Water Board buildings. Stride along the delightful valley with Hopes Burn to your right. As you reach the few houses at

Hopes Reservoir

West Hopes, wind left for two or three steps and then continue uphill on a wide dirt track, keeping parallel, but well above, the Hopes Burn down to your right. As you go look out for the slope of the grass-clad dam wall and then you spot the interesting ladder-like stone trough and buildings at its top, and at its base, as the water flows out of the reservoir for its first treatment. Notice the little bridge just below you built of fine stone. Then the blue water of the charming pool comes into view. Stroll on along the good track as it winds round a tiny bay and then goes on as a track high above the delightful reservoir.

2 Follow the track as it turns away from the water and begins to ascend between the slopes of Trindle Bonny and Windy Law. Just before the ford where the Hopes Water crosses the track on its way to the reservoir, turn right to walk a grassy path. Cross the burn on stones and begin to climb a steeply sloping broad track. It soon levels and is a pleasure to walk along the west side of the reservoir, with trees and a good wire fence to your right. It continues on parallel with another arm of the reservoir, with steep heather slopes to the left and deciduous woodland dropping down to the water below, the trees the haunt of songbirds. The way then winds away from the water and finally makes an acute right turn and drops steeply down, a short way, to the narrow valley of the Sting Bank Burn.

3 Step across and zigzag up the grassy slope, ahead, to a path leading, right, to a gate in deciduous woodland. At first the path is narrow and several young trees have fallen. Pick your way round these with care and then go on along the lovely way, through young birch. Below some of the trees to your right stands a sturdy fence, then more trees and finally the waters of the reservoir. Eventually the good path leaves the trees and you can look across the water to its dam and several buildings. Finally the path brings you to a stile over the fence on your right. It continues down a slope and then by steps cut into the turf by many walkers and leads you to the side of the dam.

4 Do not cross, unless you wish to explore. Follow the now glorious wide, grassy track going downhill, with

Walk 9

½ km

½ mile

40

the wall of the dam to your right. The way winds on down easing the gradient and passing through more superb birch woodland. Cross the bridge over the Hopes Burn. As you go you might spot roe deer up on the hill slope to your right. The track brings you to a gate and stile out into the open valley and the track continues on to West Hopes. Beyond the stile beside the gate, carry on ahead soon to return to where you have parked.

Roe Deer

Practicals

Type of walk: *The reservoir is a delight to walk round.*

Total distance: 4½ miles/7.5km

Time: 2–3 hours

Maps: OS Explorer 345/Landranger 66

Walk 10

Meikle Says Law

Park in a layby, opposite a gate, grid ref 613637. Access this from the village of Gifford by the B6355. After 6.5km/4 miles, where the road turns sharp left, go ahead along an unclassified road for 1.1km/3/4mile.

Before the heather flowers and transforms the moorland, it can seem a dour and lonely place for a walk. But even in early spring it is surprising how much life can be spotted. Watch out for **mountain hares**, still completely white in late spring, racing down through the heather, not yet having assumed their summer habit. A short quiet sit on a heather mound might tempt a lizard to cross a gap between plants. Wheatears flit about the stones of old grouse butts, revealing their white rumps as they go. Grouse disturb you, as you climb, shouting 'Go back. Go back' as they fly off. The haunting calls of curlews can be heard and as you near the summit listen for the high piping call of golden plovers. When you cross the Faseny Burn you might see dippers, grey wagtails and common sandpiper.

Faseny Water

1 Cross the road and beyond the gate, descend a wide steepish track, to pass to the right of Faseny Cottage. Follow the track round right for a few steps and then ford the Faseny Water. There was once a bridge that crossed the narrow burn, below the cottage, but sadly it no longer exists. Maybe you'll need to take off your boots and wade through the water if the

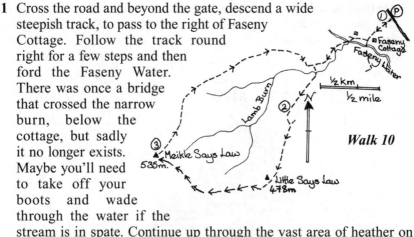

Walk 10

stream is in spate. Continue up through the vast area of heather on the wide reinforced track, with the Lamb Burn down to your left, and climb steadily until you reach a T-junction. Turn left here and follow this wide track as it descends to the Easter Lamb Burn, which you will also have to wade or jump across. Continue through this little green oasis and then begin climbing again.

2 When the distinct track begins to fade, head on up following a faint vehicle track, which appears to move to one side or the other of a large drainage trench. Where much higher ground is reached, heather becomes scarce and the ground gravelly. Listen here for golden plover, curlew and the ubiquitous grouse. On spotting the boundary fence on Little Says Law, continue towards it. Turn right before it and after a short boggy area, pick up a narrow path through the heather, which keeps about 20yds/18m to the right of the fence. Look for spreads of 'normal feed' and 'medicated feed' placed regularly by the side of the 'path' for the grouse, preparing for the breeding season after the long winter months. After a peaty boggy area where you need to step from tuft of grass to the next one, the path improves and soon arrives at a bend in the fence. Wind right just before the corner and carry on up, the gap between you and the fence wider now. Soon you can see the trig point on Meikle Says Law. Aim for it and enjoy the splendid views. It is the highest hill at just over 1700ft/535m in the northern Lammermuirs.

3 Leave the top in a north-east direction on a faint path, keeping well up on the ridge – don't drift right into ankle twisting heather. Stay up on the indistinct path, which eventually becomes a clearer track marked by vehicles down Sheil Rig. The way gradually drifts east past various grouse butts over Dun Side and then goes by more grouse butts to join a better track. At the junction of tracks, met almost at the beginning of the walk, turn left and descend to cross the Faseny Water once more. Turn right, then wind left and climb the steep track to rejoin your vehicle.

Mountain Hare

Practicals

Type of walk: *Suitable for seasoned hill walkers who can read a map and use a compass. There is no road walking but lots of indistinct paths through the heather to be 'discovered'. Some very good vehicle tracks. The two burns might cause problems after heavy rain. The tracks shown on the Explorer map which are used on this walk exist only in parts.*

Total distance: 6½ miles/10.5km
Time: 3–4 hours
Maps: OS Explorer 345/Landranger 67

Walk 11

Priestlaw Hill and Whiteadder Reservoir

Park in a layby opposite to the access road to Priestlaw Farm, grid ref 643644. To reach this, take the B6355 from Gifford, turning east round its village church and continuing east for 8 miles/13km to the parking layby.

The **Lammermuirs** at first sight seem formidable, a depressing patchwork of burnt heather but the remoteness and the patchwork patterns created by burning the heather grow on you. In summer when the sun shines they welcome you and soon become friends. In autumn the heather, colour and perfume, is a delight. In winter when snow descends they become dramatic and demand great care on your walks. In spring the new shoots, the young lambs and the teeming but secretive wild life are enchanting.

1 Cross the road and walk down the narrow access road as it descends, winds and then rises a little. Soon you have a fine view of the bridge across the Faseny Water as it enters the reservoir. Turn right, well before the bridge, along a gated track, signposted 'Penshiel', and climb steadily

Priestlaw Hill

towards two cottages. In the fields green plovers wheel and dive, oyster catchers pipe and curlews call. Curve round, left, towards the cottages and just before them, take a signposted gate on the right to carry on along a delightful green track. The pleasing way moves out into a fine valley, with Penshiel Hill to the right and Priestlaw left. Go past the Chapel Stone on your right, with a ruined stone building on either side of the track.

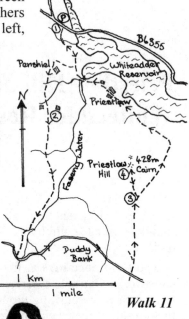

Walk 11

2 About the pasture, particularly the wetter areas, Canada and Greylag Geese feed and honk. After 2 miles/3.4km the delightful track crosses the Faseny Water by a stone bridge and then the path joins a narrow unclassified road.

Canada Geese

Turn left and begin the steady ascent of the almost traffic-free road. After ¾ mile/1.3km it drops a little to cross the narrow Craig burn. Then climb to the brow on the little road and take the signposted gate on the left. This gives access to another wide grassy trod, a joy to walk. Where it splits, go ahead, taking the right branch. This becomes rougher in parts and peaty in places and then improves again.

3 After ½ mile/1km and where you can spot the cairn on Priestlaw Hill, watch out for a narrower path, left. Follow this easy-to-walk way, ascend a grassy trod and then stroll through heather on a narrow path, which soon brings you to an ancient cairn with an interesting walled area of grass beside it. The views of the surrounding hills are very good. Walk on to a second cairn from where there is a superb view of the reservoir down below and of the many hills around.

4 Return by the same route to the main track and turn left. The lovely path is a delight, with only one rather wet patch. It continues high above the south side of the reservoir, descending steadily. Go through a gate and then pass through the outbuildings of Priestlaw Farm. Head on to cross the footbridge over the Faseny water, viewed at the outset, and bear right to begin the climb up the access track to where you have parked.

Oystercatchers

Practicals

Type of walk: *Very, very pleasant. It is a walk through the lower Lammermuirs that retains a pleasing air of remoteness and isolation.*

Total distance: 6½ miles/10.5km

Time: 3–4 hours

Maps: OS Explorer 345/Landranger 67

Walk 12

Watch Water Reservoir and Twin Law

Park in the car park on the north side of the reservoir, grid ref 663567. Access this from the pretty village of Longformacus, which lies between Duns and Gifford. If travelling from Duns, turn left before the bridge over the River Dye. Continue along the narrow road, part of the Southern Upland Way (SUW). After Rawburn farm outbuildings bear right with the road, soon to drive above the reservoir to your left. Carry on along the dam to reach the car park (and fishing club café in summer).

Stretching from Portpatrick to Cocksburnpath on the North Sea Coast, the **Southern Upland Way** (SUW) was the first of Scotland's many cross country walking routes. The SUW is also used by cyclists and horse riders.

The **Lammermuir Hills** cover some 150 sq miles.. They are not Munros or even Corbetts. Their main tops are around 1600-1700 ft/500m but they should be treated with respect in the winter and all the usual safety precautions should be taken. At the right time of year, as you walk these lovely hills listen, and look, for lapwings, curlews, redshank, oyster catchers and red grouse.

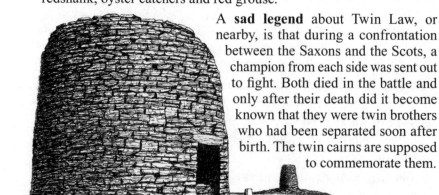

A **sad legend** about Twin Law, or nearby, is that during a confrontation between the Saxons and the Scots, a champion from each side was sent out to fight. Both died in the battle and only after their death did it become known that they were twin brothers who had been separated soon after birth. The twin cairns are supposed to commemorate them.

Cairns, Twin Law
Summit (in snow)

48

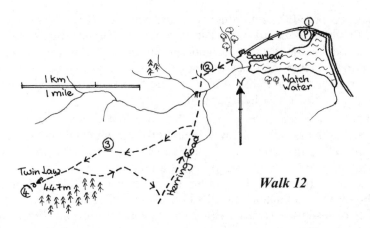

Walk 12

1 Set off from the car park and continue along the SUW, a narrow met-alled road, with the reservoir to your left. It passes through rough moorland to reach, after ½ mile, Scarlaw farm, snug beside its long shelterbelt of fine beech and ash. Wade a small stream, Dam Howe, and carry on to step over another stream soon to reach a signposted junction of tracks.

2 Turn left (still on the SUW) to join the Herring Road, along which were carried salted herrings from ports on the east coast to the Scottish Border villages. Descend steadily to the Watch Water Burn hurrying to join the reservoir. To your right is a little path leading to a plank footbridge. Just before this, to the right of the main path, is a small monument to John Dippie, a gamekeeper from Rawfold Estate. Below is his well. Once over the footbridge return to the track and begin to ascend, passing a walled area to your right, which once enclosed a small plantation of trees. Continue on to a signposted gate and a fence. Do not go through the gate but turn right to step through a short boggy area and stroll the lovely grassy sheep-nibbled path, uphill over the heather moorland, with the fence on your left and still on the SUW.

3 Watch out as you go for a distant view of the first of the cairns on Twin Law. Follow the signed track as it bends a bit and begins to climb more steeply before reaching a gate in a wall on the left, with a step stile beside it. Beyond, walk the continuing path over the moorland towards the huge cairn ahead and then the second one comes into view. Soon you reach the summit, with a white trig point between the two barrel-shaped cairns. Both rise out of large circles of stones and have easy steps to access south-facing seats recessed into the structures. Look for the book in the first seat, in a polythene bag, where previous walkers

49

have recorded their comments. There are several pencils in the bag with which to record your visit, if you wish. Perhaps this is the place for your picnic. From here you can look over the rolling moorland to England and the massive Cheviot. To its right you can see, much nearer, the Eildon Hills. In the opposite direction you can view a long stretch of the lonely Lammermuirs.

4 Then start your return, watching for your first view of the reservoir, nestling in the valley below. About 200yds/180m from the cairns, and well before the stile, take a wide track going off right, through the heather, soon to wind round beside an old quarry. At the Y-junction take the left branch descending a rougher way, beside conifers. Go through a small gate in a wall and walk a winding track used by vehicles to reach the Herring Road where you turn left and stroll on to reach the gate you ignored on the way up. This time, pass through to join the SUW and continue to the footbridge. Shortly afterwards, turn right to stride over the moorland to the car park.

Lapwing

Practicals

Type of walk: *Very pleasing, through dramatic hills. There are good distinct paths and tracks, and the route has several waymarks. After rain expect some wet patches.*

Total distance: 6½ miles/10km

Time: 3–4 hours

Maps: OS Explorer 345/Landranger 67

Walk 13

Abbey St Bathans

Park in the public car park, beside the Whiteadder Water and behind The Riverside restaurant, grid ref 762619. Access this from Gifford, Grantshouse or Cockburnspath.

The tiny **village of Abbey St Bathans** lies beside the Whiteadder Water deep in the heart of the Lammermuir Hills. It has a pretty church, a thriving sawmill, a fish farm and a few houses. You pass the name-plate of the village and in a few minutes you have left the village behind, a tiny, fragmented settlement on minor roads, five miles from Duns.

The **magnificent high-level footbridge** carries the Southern Upland Way over the burn and the six-foot high depth marker beside the wide vehicle track over the ford are testament to the sudden flooding that has occurred along this stretch of river over the centuries.

Abbey St Bathans Church

The settlement has never **been home to an abbey**, though in about the year 1200 a small Cistercian priory of 12 nuns was founded here by Countess Ada of Dunbar. The site was chosen because it was believed that a visiting missionary, St Bathan, a follower of St Columba in the late 500s, erected a chapel here.

Edin's Hall Broch dates from the Iron Age. It stands on rising ground on the site of a much

51

earlier settlement. Its diameter measures about 80ft/25m and its walls vary in thickness. Some stand around 4 ft/1.5m high and would have been higher if, in the past, most of the buildings had not been dismantled to construct drystone walls.

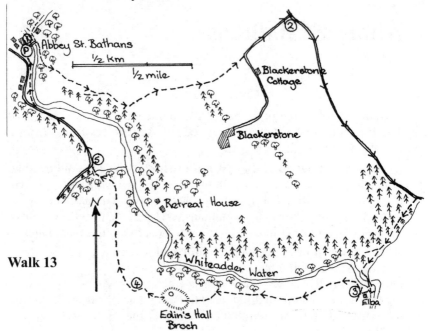

Walk 13

1 From the car park, cross the high footbridge or the wide vehicle track over the ford. Turn right immediately to ascend a lovely grassy track up through fine deciduous woodland, with the wide hurrying burn down to your right. Follow the path as it emerges from the trees and continues ahead, gently descending through gorse and down a grassy slope to a stile onto a wide reinforced track. Turn left and climb up the hedged way. At first it can be wet and muddy but it soon improves and climbs steadily, with pastures to the left and mixed woodland to the right. Ignore a turning right, and go on along the reinforced track as directed by the waymarked post. Enjoy the wide views across to the right and then go by Blackerstone Cottage, where the track becomes tarmacked.

2 At the unclassified road, almost traffic-free, turn right following the waymark, and begin your ¾ mile/1.4km walk, which soon begins to descend through more pleasing woodland. At the foot of the hill there is a sign directing you, right, along a potholed track for Edin's Hall

Broch. The track passes through woodland. At the Y-junction take the left branch and descend through the trees to the foot of a white and yellow footbridge that uses the abutments of an older bridge. The bridge lies slightly to your left along a short footpath. You are asked that only two people at a time use the bridge and not to jump up and down while crossing. Below the bridge, to the left, the burn eddies round two large pools and tumbles between the two in a fine white-topped cascade, overshadowed by craggy cliffs. Descend from the bridge, walk ahead, with a house at Elba to your left. Go on for a few steps to take a gate, on the right, which has a notice asking you to close it after use.

3 Walk ahead and then climb left to make a large arc, right, round a huge clump of gorse. This brings you to the top of a high bank along which you stroll, with the river down to your right. Enjoy this pleasing airy way. Climb an easy step-stile over the wall ahead and continue on. Go on across the next field and climb a similar stile. Walk on along the third field to a tall metal kissing gate. This is difficult and few walkers will be able to pass through with their rucksacks on, unless they climb up three rungs of the metal construction and then step round right at the same height, moving the gate at the same time. Beyond, look ahead to see a narrow path slanting gently up the steep slope, left, on which the broch stands and ascend to the lip of the hill. Ahead lies spectacular Edin's Hall Broch and many other circles and arrangements of stones. Wander around this superb, atmospheric site and read the information boards. Then follow the distinct narrow path that leads over what might be an ancient rampart and slopes down before rising again across the field to a gate in the far top corner. As you go, look right, down into the valley to see The Retreat, with its fine circular section, built for the Earl of Wemyss in 1784 as a hunting lodge and a retreat.

Wood Anemones

4 Beyond the gate, walk uphill, beside the fence on your left to climb a stile over it, close by a sign-post. From here stretches a glorious path, half a mile long, descending at first, and then levelling half way up the vast sloping heath-like pasture, covered in spring by an enormous carpet of wood anemones.

Here clumps of primroses, violets and celandines add colour to the scene. Follow the little path to the edge of a belt of woodland and then where it drops left and continues beside Eller Burn, a tributary of the Whiteadder Water, to a footbridge deep in a leafy hollow. Cross and walk up some steep steps through more woodland to reach a sharp bend in the road to the village. By the signpost stands an extraordinary sign, which reads "TOOT".

5 Turn right and walk down towards the village, facing oncoming traffic. Before the final bend in the valley, look for wooden steps leading down to the side of the river. Turn left to walk beside the hurrying river and rejoin the road just opposite the wood yard (thus avoiding traffic on the sharp bend). Turn right and walk on the few yards to the car park on the right.

Bluetit

Practicals

Type of walk: *Very satisfactory. Quite delightful. Good paths and tracks with some road walking.*

Total distance: 5½ miles/9km
Time: 3 hours
Maps: OS Explorer 346/Landranger 67

Walk 14

Duns Castle Nature Reserve

Park in any available space along Newton Street (A6105), or in the car park, south, off the A-road, grid ref 784539.

The original **Duns Castle**, a pele tower, was built around 1320 by the Earl of Moray, the nephew of King Robert the Bruce. By 1697 the castle had come into the possession of the Hay family when the Earl of Tweeddale bought it for his son William Hay of Drumelzier. It has belonged to the Hay family ever since, each generation enlarging and improving it, transforming it along the years to what you see today. Sadly it is not open to the public.

In 1377 the Earl of Northumberland invaded Scotland. Having met little resistance, he rested his men at Duns. The townspeople realising the Earl was off his guard concocted **"a kind of rattle, made of dried skins distended round ribs of wood that were bended into a semi-circular form and fixed at the end of long poles".** When these

*Duns
Castle*

were shaken they made a terrible noise, causing the horses to bolt. The Earl's men fled, routed by the local people. In 1544, 1545 and 1558 the English razed Duns to the ground. In 1650 Cromwell placed a garrison in the town.

The **Mercat Cross** stands on the south side of Duns market square. For a Scottish town or village it was a symbol of its trading status. Before the 19th century it was a place where punishment or public humiliation took place.

1 From where you have parked, walk east along the A-road and wind left up the A6112. Where the road bears right, go ahead and then under a fine arch, passing North Lodge on your right. Continue along the estate road of the castle, until you reach a low memorial cairn on your right. The plate on top says that it is dedicated to John Duns Scotus, an influential theologian of the middle ages, who was born at this site in 1216. The cairn was erected September 1966, the seventh centenary of his birth. The cairn also says that the word 'dunce' comes from his name. Just before a second fine archway, beyond the cairn, wind right on a good track, leading to Hen Poo Lake and the Duns Castle Nature Reserve.

2 You will wish to dawdle beside the lake, enjoying its charm, and the ducks and geese that inhabit it. Towards the far end of the lake, ignore a private track on the right and go ahead into deciduous woodland, with an understory of rhododendrons and continue on where the track winds round the foot of the lake. At the signpost turn right to walk through the woodland to come beside the delightful Mill Pond, where there is a seat from which to enjoy, perhaps, a heron and goosanders. Once beyond the lovely pool, turn left to walk the signposted Colonel's walk, a long track beside a little stream. Dawdle on through the narrow tree-lined valley sometimes with conifers to your right and deciduous

Walk 14

trees to the left. Then cross a footbridge over a stream and climb steps to a seat. Go on along a narrow path through more forestry, with the stream chuckling to your right. The track is littered with last year's beech leaves and there are several seats to enjoy the quiet ambience of the woodland. Turn left at the signpost to walk the Green Ride, through St Mary's Glade.

3   At the T-junction take the track to the right, signed 'To the Hide'. This lovely tree-lined way takes you along the opposite side of the lake to that taken earlier, passing the convenient bird watching hide on the way. Where the path turns away from the lake at the cross of tracks, with a cottage away to the right, go ahead towards a gate and continue beside a field, on your right. Then the track passes, on the left, some buildings; walk on along the waymarked track beside the Castle's extensive grounds, with a fine view of the splendid building to your left. The track ends at the A6105. Turn left and walk past the Sports Centre and Duns School. Go by the ornate main gate to the castle and continue on a short way to reach your vehicle.

Goosanders

Practicals

Type of walk: *A very pleasing walk through glorious woodland and beside a fine lake and pond.*

Total distance: 4 miles/6.5km
Time: 2½ hours
Map: OS Explorer 346/Landranger 67

Walk 15

Lauder

Park in the Main Street of Lauder, grid ref 530475.

The attractive **historic village of Lauder** sits astride the A68 and through its main street pass innumerable cars, wagons and other vehicles. The noise and bustle can be almost unbearable at times. But a short distance away you can ascend onto the lonely moorland and the only sound is the soughing of the wind, and calls of curlews at the right time of year. The A68 follows the oldest established route between Edinburgh and England, along which has tramped many an army over the centuries. Today the Southern Upland Way passes through the town on its 212 miles journey, from coast to coast.

The Tolbooth, Lauder

1 Go down Market Street, with the 14th century tollbooth to your left, and the unique 17th century church, to your right. Once past the church turn right down Mill Wynd. Cross the road bridge over Lauder Burn and turn right. Keep to the left of the ruined mill heading for a Southern Upland Way (SUW) sign. Follow the good grassy track steadily uphill to a seat by a gate. Pause here to look across to the Lammermuirs, sheltering Lauder and Thirlestane Castle below. Go through the gate and carry on. Ignore a signposted right

C.M.Isherwood

58

turn (useful if the weather has changed and you need to shorten the walk). Beyond the fence to your left is Lauder golf course.

2 Walk on along the narrow path, with a very steep slope to your right. Deep in the narrow valley, meanders the Lauder Burn. On the other side of the burn the ground slopes up equally steeply to sheep pasture and moorland above. Go past two small cairns made by local young people and follow the SUW as it begins to descend gently. It then swings left and continues to an easily spotted ladderstile. At this point leave the SUW and descend a green path to begin a steep descent, or use the large zigzagging path down by the wall to the burn and then carry on beside the water to a pleasing footbridge. This is a pretty corner, where sheep and their lambs congregate, the gorse flowers and in the marshy areas grow yellow irises.

3 Once over the bridge, follow a signposted green path to climb the slope ahead. There are several paths to choose from and eventually you climb straight up to a prominent waymarked post. Bear right at the post and walk along the grassy path towards the right side of Cuckoo Wood, a mixture of Scots pine and rather badly wind blown larch. Once past, keep on half left to come beside the wall on the left side of the high moorland. Remain beside the wall as it continues and then where it begins to descend. Step over any little marshy places and cross a tiny stream on convenient stones against the wall. Pass through a large area of gorse to arrive at a sign-posted gate.

4 Beyond, turn right and drop down a large arable pasture towards the burn. Keep parallel with the wall until the path curves left along the side of the burn. Go through a gate and on to cross a footbridge. Then head up the stepped path up a short slope to reach a wide terraced path, with large patches of gorse covering the steep slope above. Head on the delightful way as it gradually descends. Cross the stream and a marshy area on a long boardwalk to continue on the far side of the burn. The pleasing way then continues through

Walk 15

59

delectable mixed woodland, with the burn burbling beside you. This sheltered area is full of wild flowers and the haunt of small birds. The track eventually becomes tarmacked and arrives at the foot of Mill Wynd walked earlier. Turn left and walk into Lauder.

Iris

Practicals

Type of walk: *Very satisfactory. A steady climb on the SUW and then a descent to a pretty stretch of the Lauder Burn. The return is equally enjoyable with a walk high over the moor, well signposted and then beside the burn as it passes through deciduous woodland.*

Total distance: 3½ miles/5.5km

Time: 2 hours

Maps: OS Explorer 338/Landranger 73

Walk 16

Ewes Castle, Stow

Park in a grassy area on the right side, at the east end of Lugate Bridge, grid ref 450434. Access this from the village of Stow, turning west off the A7, then crossing the bridge over the Gala Water and continuing to the T-junction where you turn left. Drive on for 1mile/1.5km and park well tucked in to the wall of the bridge.

Lugate Bridge carried the old stage road across Lugate Water, just before the burn joins Gala Water on its way to the Tweed. Another attractive bridge is passed if you approach the village of Stow from the south on the A7. This is an **old pack horse bridge** across the Gala Water which was built in 1655. It was the first bridge over the Gala and it linked Stow with the main route between Edinburgh and Galashiels. Before then everyone had to use fords.

On top of Ewes Castle

1 Go through the gate and walk up the track beside your parking area. To the left flows the Lugate Water and in the bushes beside it a sedge

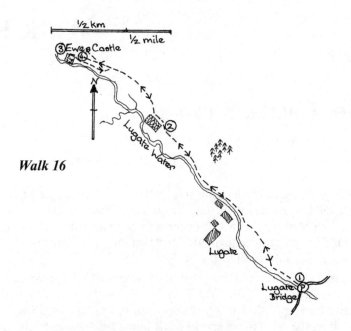

½ km

½ mile

③ Ewes Castle

④

N

Walk 16

Lugate Water

②

Lugate

Lugate Bridge ①Ⓟ

warbler sings enthusiastically. To the right are the lower slopes of Stagehall Hill, where cattle graze. Continue through a gate and on along the winding track, with an arable crop to the left. Go through another gate to walk close to the burn, shadowed by willows, with gorse towering far up the hill to your right. Then the track moves out into the open and the area has been well used by cows and sheep. Across the burn stands the settlement of Lugate.

2 Carry on along the track to wind right of a fenced disused fish farm to come to a metal gate. If it is tied very tightly it is easier to climb over it. Walk on along the little path, distinct but stony for much of the way. Eventually the path improves for a short way and you can see the large grassy hump of Ewes Castle ahead. As you pass below the steep slopes of Cribbilaw Hill, on the right, notice the large patches of bell heather that cover the scree. To your left lies a flat area of reeds and rough grass among which flowers meadow sweet and ragged robin. Walk on keeping left at a Y-junction to come beside the fence that encloses the ruin and climb the hurdle gate at the corner.

3 Step across a short damp way to climb over the remains of the low wall and go on to stand at the foot of the grassy mound. Ascend the side, with care, and stand on the little flat top. In July it is covered with many flowers. There is a hollow in the top filled with a few boulders. Pause

here and enjoy the delightful view up the valley, with steep lonely hills stretching away into the far distance, making it a good strategic position when it was occupied. In spite of it now being a tiny ruin the site is most atmospheric.

4 To return, retrace your steps through the valley.

Sedge Warbler

Practicals

Type of walk: *Short and very pleasant.*

Total distance: 3 miles/5km
Time: 1½ hours
Maps OS Explorer 338/ Landranger 73

Walk 17

Kilcoulter Bridge and Heriot Water

Park on the large verge on the right, west, to the north side of Kilcoulter Bridge, grid ref 409529. Access this by the A7 from Stow in the direction of Edinburgh. Turn left at Heriot onto the B709 and at Sandyknowe take the left turn and continue to Kilcoulter Bridge.

The very pretty **monkeyflower**, *Mimulus guttatus*, yellow with red spots is a garden escapee. It has naturalized beside streams and flowers between June and August. It comes in various colour forms, plain yellow, yellow with red spots, and a lovely clear orange.

Monkeyflower

The male **yellowhammer's song** is often given from its favourite song-post such as the top of a fir tree or hawthorn bush. The cock has bright yellow and chestnut plumage, which is easy to spot. Its song has been described as a 'little-bit-of-bread-and-no-cheese', the Scottish version as 'deil-deil-deil-tak ye', and it may be heard from late February until the middle of August and sometimes much later.

1 Cross the Kilcoulter bridge over the Heriot Water and wind round left, to take, right, a tarmacked narrow road, signed to Corsehope. Down to your left flows the Corsehope burn, edged in summer with yellow

Yellowhammer

Kilcoulter Bridge

monkeyflowers. Enjoy the verges of the pleasing road, which are lined with flowers and in the trees look for goldfinch, willow warbler and yellowhammer. The hills on either side slope steeply down and ahead you can see more high hills. Continue gently ascending to reach Corsehope House. Walk on over the cattle grid and past the fine flower garden of the house to see a series of pools, with water being channelled between each through pipes.

2 Return to the gate, on the left, before the cattle grid. Beyond, climb the grassy track with a row of low trees to the left and rolling sloping pastures to the right. Then the trees are left behind and the good track begins its zigzagging descent through flower meadows, easing the steepness. Eventually you arrive at a fence, where you turn right to continue through a gate and along a level way. Soon you can see the Heriot Water through the trees on the left.

3 At the White Bridge you need to make a choice on your return route. Some walkers will, in summer, wish to ignore the bridge and enjoy the challenge of continuing ahead on the very overgrown path, ¾ mile/1.3km

Walk 17

long, through lush vegetation under woodland trees. The path winds and turns, comes very close to the Heriot Water and then goes on under lofty spruce. It passes through tall grass, goes to the right of a fence and finally brings you to stone steps over a wall, with a gap beside them, to join the road. Turn left to rejoin your vehicle. Other walkers may find the path through the woods too daunting and will prefer to cross the White Bridge and walk past the MacFie Hall to the B709. Turn right here and continue to the junction with the unclassified road at Sandyknowe. Turn acute right and walk on towards Kilcoulter Bridge.

Wild roses

Practicals

Type of walk: *Very satisfactory. Some narrow road walking. Wide grassy trods and then the choice of a narrow path through lush woodland or along more quiet roads.*

Total distance: 3 miles/5km or 4 miles/6.5km if you use the road.

Time: 2–3 hours

OS Explorer 345/Landranger 73

Eddleston

Park in Station Road in Eddleston, grid ref 242472. Access this by turning left off the A703 from Peebles into Old Manse Road at the sign 'Lyne via Meldons', then left into Station Road.

Eddleston is a delightful conservation village only 4 ½ miles/7.4m from Peebles and 18 miles/24km south of Edinburgh. It lies in a valley, which provides one of the few routes through the Moorfoot hills.

After a battle in 1189 the village passed to **Edulf, the son of Ultred**, both English names indicating the influence that England was having in lowland Scotland. The village would have been known as Edulf's town or 'toun' and hence Eddleston.

From 1926 the fine **Barony Castle** was a hotel. Today most of it is a conference centre. Another part of the charming building is the Scottish Ambulance College and you may pass several ambulances parked beside the track, almost at the start of the walk.

Cottage, Eddleston

1 Walk out of Station Road and cross to take an access track signposted to Barony Castle. Walk up the tarmacked way and before the large entrance gates to the Castle, bear right as directed by the signpost. Wind round left with the road. Ignore the signpost on the right, directing you into woodland, and continue on the narrow road. Here you might see a spotted flycatcher darting out from its favourite perch to snap up a fly and then returning to the same observation post. Pass the dramatic Castle on your left and then the parked ambulances just before the end of the tarmac. Ignore a path dropping left and go on, gently descending a tree-lined unsurfaced track.

Walk 18

2 Wind round left with the track to cross the burn and pass between a house on either side. Climb steadily and wind round right, Bunny Corner, with the track. Head on with a fence to the left and enjoy the fine view, left, over the fields towards Peebles with the Tweedsmuir Hills beyond. At the next gate marked private, turn left, following waymarks along a fine grassy track, hedged and fenced, which climbs steadily. Wind right at the top of the hill. Beyond the next gate, carry on left along a narrower way through birch woodland. Then follow the lovely way through more glorious deciduous trees and shrubs to reach a signpost. Here turn sharp right in the direction of Shiplaw.

3 Step over Fairydean Burn and go through a gate to walk through fields with a wall to the right. Beyond the next gate walk on with a walled beech and pine woodland to the right. At the four-armed signpost take the right turn for Darnhall along a short, wide track, through conifers, with a fence to your right. Leave the trees behind and begin your descent on a wide track down over open grassland, with a fine view of Dundreich.

4 Wind right to pass through the extensive outbuildings of Darnhall Mains to take the next left turn, tarmacked and descending below the fine house. Continue down the narrow way to cross the Eddleston

Water and go on to reach the A703, the road to Edinburgh. Cross with care and walk ahead into bushes where the signpost is hidden. Join a narrow track and walk right along the tree-lined way. Soon this becomes an obvious road, the old road to Edinburgh. It continues, traffic-free and lined with limes, into Eddleston. Cross the road just before you reach the Horseshoe Inn and turn right down the road signposted to Lyne via The Meldons. Cross the bridge over the Eddleston Water and turn left into Station Road. You may like to walk along this pretty way to see the pleasing bridge over the flower-lined burn.

Spotted Flycatcher

Practicals

Type of walk: *A fairly short, often level, walk through quiet delightful countryside. Well signposted all the way.*

Total distance: 4 miles/6.5km
Time: 2–3 hours
Maps: OS Explorer 337/Landranger 73

Walk 19

Cloich Hills from Newlands

Park in the large layby opposite Newlands church, grid ref 161466. Access this by the A72 from Peebles and after 7 miles turn right onto the B7059 to drive 3 miles along the Lyne Water Valley.

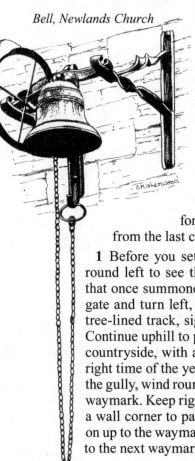

Bell, Newlands Church

This is a fine circular walk through the rounded grass-covered **Cloich Hills**, where you are serenaded by many skylarks and delighted by the call of the curlew. Here on the lonely slopes innumerable sheep graze. The whole walk is on fine grassy tracks and paths from where there are wonderful views down to the Lyne Valley and towards the Broughton Heights. On your return you can enjoy a long backdrop of the Pentland Hills, with Arthur's Seat at the far end. The final joy of the walk is visiting the fort and enclosure, on Whiteside Hill, dating from the last century BC.

1 Before you set off, go into the churchyard and wind round left to see the ancient bell high on an outside wall that once summoned people to services. Then leave by the gate and turn left, south. After a few steps stroll left up a tree-lined track, signed as a Scottish Rights of Way route. Continue uphill to pass through a large metal gate into open countryside, with a deep gully to your right, where, at the right time of the year, many yellow iris flower. At the top of the gully, wind round to the right, following the Tweed Trails waymark. Keep right of Whiteside cottage and head towards a wall corner to pass through a waymarked wall gap. Head on up to the waymark on the top of a low ridge, then descend to the next waymark in a hollow.

2 Go on up beside the wall on your left, climbing quite steeply to a T-junction of tracks. Wind right to follow the pleasing trod contouring the western slopes of Whiteside Hill with a fine view down to the Lyne Water and ahead to the Broughton

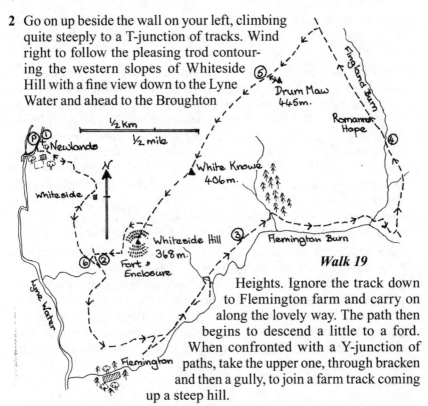

Walk 19

Heights. Ignore the track down to Flemington farm and carry on along the lovely way. The path then begins to descend a little to a ford. When confronted with a Y-junction of paths, take the upper one, through bracken and then a gully, to join a farm track coming up a steep hill.

3 Walk on the terraced track to ford, or jump, another little burn and then wind on round the foot of a small conifer plantation. Follow the waymark on the corner of the walled trees and go on to cross the next ford and climb the steep slope beyond. At a waymarked cross of tracks, turn left to a seat – just the place for your lunch. Then continue on the satisfying track into Romanno Hope, with the slopes of Hag Law, 1350m/446m, to the right and of Drum Maw,1347ft/ 445m, to the left. The track descends gently to a gate, the grassy edges colourful with lousewort, common speedwell, eyebright, and the ubiquitous white bedstraw and tormentil.

4 Go on to ford the Fingland Burn and climb steadily the continuing track through the bracken, to come to a gate into a conifer plantation. Do not go through but climb steeply left, up beside a fence and a wall to your right. Pause as you go, to look right towards West Linton and beyond to the Pentland Hills stretching along the horizon to Arthur's Seat. To your left grows bracken and as you climb this is replaced by cushions of moss on which thrives more white bedstraw. Soon the wall turns down right and, to the left, a little path leads you on for a few steps to the cairned summit of Drum Maw.

5 From the wall corner, carry on along the grassy track and follow it as it climbs to White Knowe, 1320ft/406m. From the summit, look ahead for a dramatic view of the ring dykes and enclosures of the fort on Whiteside Hill. Continue from the summit of White Knowe by the track keeping slightly right to descend to a col, where there is a cross of tracks. Climb up to the magical fort and wind round its ring dykes. You will want to spend some time at this site. Then return down the same slope to the col and turn left on a good track that slants steadily downhill to come beside a wall. Walk left and follow it, past a gate, and on along the lower slopes of Whiteside Hill, until it turns down right. Turn down with the wall and descend steeply to the trod taken earlier.

6 Ford the little stream and bear right to climb to the waymark on the hill. Descend from here to a wall corner and follow the wall, keeping it on your right. At the corner with another wall, go through the waymarked gap and then pass in front of Whiteside cottage. Continue down its access track, wind left and go on down, with the gully to your left, to go through the large metal gate. Beyond, descend the tree-lined track and continue to the B-road. Turn right to the church and the parking area.

Curlews

Practicals

Type of walk: *A wonderful walk into magnificent Border hill country. Good tracks and paths for all the way.*

Complete distance: 7 miles/11.3km
Time: 4–5 hours
Maps: OS Explorer336/Landranger 72

Trahenna Hill above Broughton

Park in the Walkers' car park, grid ref 120375. Access this by leaving the northern end of the pleasing village of Broughton, which sits astride the A701. Just beyond the speed de-restriction sign, turn right up a narrow easy-to-miss lane lined with fine beech and lime trees. Bear left and then right round Broughton Place farm and continue up the hill, lined with more magnificent trees. Drive past dramatic Broughton Place and where the road winds right, go ahead along a reinforced track to the parking area before a shepherd's cottage.

This walk takes you on paths and tracks walked by many generations of shepherds through and over the rounded grassy tops of **Broughton Heights**.

John Buchan was born in 1875. He wrote many novels, the most famous starring the secret agent Richard Hannay. *The Thirty-Nine*

Sheep Fold,
Stobo Hopehead

Steps was, and still is, the most widely read and the best known. In recognition of all his work he received the title of Baron Tweedsmuir. The **John Buchan Way** (JBW) is a route from Peebles to Broughton. It is approximately 13 miles/22km in length and is waymarked in both directions. It was opened in 2003 and is named after the famous writer who had many associations with the area.

1 Go through the gate across the track to walk the JBW, a delightful level grassy way heading towards a clump of scots pine, with lonely hill slopes all around. Once past the trees the track descends a little to the Hollows Burn. Look left for a pool on the burn and then take a small footbridge, or ford the tiny stream. Head on uphill on the clear track through the Broughton Valley where mountain thyme, bird's foot trefoil, white bedstraw and rock-rose line the track edge. Whinchats 'chack' from the heather. After levelling for a short way the path goes on up to a waymark at the foot of Cowiemuir Hass, where the JBW turns right.

2 Follow the good track through the heather. Go through a gate and carry on. Watch out for where the track winds right; the easy-to-miss waymark stands 100yds/91m along. Look down left to see a fine hexagonal sheep pen near the Well Burn. Soon the huge gathering shed of Stobo Hopehead farm comes into view and the track drops steadily to its rough wide access track. Turn right and a short way along look back to see the lonely dwelling with a few trees offering little shelter from the winds that sometimes sweep through the valley.

3 Remain on the rough track for about a mile, ignoring the JBW, which goes off left, until you reach a conifer plantation on the slopes, away to the left. Then look for the fine circular sheep pen with lofty Scots pine spaced pleasingly around it, perhaps the place for your lunch. Just before you reach this lovely corner, take the unsigned

Walk 20

wide grassy track climbing right and then up ahead. Soon you can see a wall high up on your left. Here the path winds, right, and begins its steepish climb of Hog Knowe (1,389ft/427m). Enjoy the superb view and then stroll on the pleasant way to cross a col before a steep climb up to Grey Yade (1,771ft/537m). Pause again to get your breath back and congratulate yourself on reaching the ridge.

4 Stride on the distinct grassy trod, with the fence to your right and don't miss where it bears half left, unmarked, to contour round to the fence ahead. Go over the fence by a small wooden hurdle and turn left up beside the fence, now on your left to reach the summit of Trahenna Hill (1783ft/549m) the highest point of the ridge and marked with a tiny cairn and a rough piece of wood. Descend by your upward path to the wooden hurdle, which you cross. Continue ahead up the slope walking a narrow path between a fence on the left and a low wall to your right. Go over a 'sort' of gate and walk ahead for a few steps to join a good track through the heather.

5 Turn left and walk on parallel with a fence to your left over Cat Cleuch Head. Then begin your steady descent on a narrower path but still beside the fence. Soon you can see, far below, the shepherd's cottage and the parking area. Here the narrow but distinct path moves away from the wall, weaves through some rocky outcrops and continues on to come close to a wall descending, right, to the valley bottom. Turn acute right and begin your descent parallel with, but well away from, the wall and go on down and down. Wind round the end of the wall and follow the clear path towards the cottage, curving round a small water catchment area on your left. Beyond, stride the pasture to go through the gate to the parking area.

Whinchat

Practicals

Type of walk: *A very satisfactory walk on good tracks and paths. There are excellent views to reward you for your ascent of the various tops on the ridge.*

Total distance: 6½ miles/ 10.5km
Time: 4–5 hours
Maps: OS Explorer 336/Landranger 72

Walk 21

Manor Head and Dollar Law

Park at the end of the metalled road up the Manor Valley, where there is a small parking space for about 4 cars, grid ref 199287. To access this take the minor road signed to Manorhead that leaves the A72, on the left, about 2 miles west of Peebles, and follow it to its end.

Dollar Law is 2635ft/817m high but is not counted as a Corbett because the land between it and the higher Broad Law does not drop the requisite 500ft/150m. It is the highest point on the circuit of the valley head, and its summit is a wide grassy plateau, providing lovely grassy walking.

There are several tracks across the Border hills with names like the **Thief's Road**, dating from the days when stealing other people's cattle (or reiving) was a way of life.

Peregrine falcons became very rare in the 1950s and 60s due to the use of organo-chlorine pesticides in sheep-dips. Fortunately these were withdrawn and since then peregrine numbers have recovered well. They frequent upland areas with cliffs and you may well see, and hear, them on this walk.

Manor Head

1 Head south-east out of the car park on a good track signed to Megget Reservoir and St. Mary's Loch. Cross the Manor Water by the foot-bridge and walk uphill below a small conifer plantation. Go through a gate onto the open hillside and continue up the gently rising grassy track, which is delightful. As you get higher the views open out, and you can see Dollar Law, your objective, across the valley to your right. Curlews call and skylarks sing. The path begins to contour and winds left above the cliffs around Bitch Cleuch; watch out for peregrines soaring above anywhere here at the valley head. Descend a short way into the upper end of the cleuch and then cross the flat area called Foulbrig. Its name is not prepossessing and indeed there are some wet places here which you will have to negotiate on the uphill side. Go through a gate and climb again, with a ditch full of bright green cushions of moss studded with starry saxifrage and ladies' smock on your right. In June there are dozens of green-veined white butterflies.

2 Leave the track at the highest point, where there is a cairn on the left, and walk right, over the short turf, to the top of Greenside Law 2081ft/643m where you reach a fence. Turn left and walk downhill beside it, enjoying the views back down the Manor Valley. Near the col at the bottom there is a gate and you may like to go through and follow the fence on the other side, over drier ground on Water Head and on to another gate where the fence goes steeply up Notman Law 2411ft/734m.

Otherwise keep on down and turn right along the path at the bottom where the fence turns; this path is very boggy across the col and round the back of Water Head, but improves as it winds up round the side of Notman Law. Cross the fence at a hurdle gate and continue on the now good path across the hillside to the col before Dollar Law, which is the great whaleback ahead. On the col the ancient track you have been following, the Thief's Road, goes through another gate. Leave it before this gate and take the wide grassy way up the ridge to the top of Dollar Law. The walking is very pleasant, over short turf,

Walk 21

and the views are splendid. The top is marked by a trig point, fence and wall junctions, and is smooth and grassy.

3 Turn right and walk beside a fence and ruined wall back towards the Manor Valley. At first there is some easy walking, then the hillside begins to get steeper. Look out for cloudberry and carpets of dwarf cornel, both in flower in June and July. The path reaches the top of the forest on the left and becomes really steep. There are many sheep tracks and by choosing carefully you can take a way down which zigzags across the slope, making the descent a little easier. Turn left on the track at the foot to return to your car.

Peregrine

Practicals

Type of walk: *Interesting. It takes you round the hills at the head of the Manor Valley, most of it is on good paths and tracks, although there is no path up Greenside Law. The Thief's Road from the col below Greenside Law to Notman Law can be very wet and you may wish to avoid the worst of this by walking on the other side of the fence. The descent from Dollar Law to the valley is very steep, and the lower part has no distinct path (because everyone takes a different route down).*

Total distance: 7 miles/11.4km

Time: 4–5 hours.

Maps: OS Explorers 336 and 337/Landrangers 72 and 73

Walk 22

Cademuir Hills and the Tweed Way

Park in the large car park south-east side of Tweed Bridge in Peebles, grid ref 251403.

The annual festival in Peebles is called the **Beltane** and involves a Common Riding. The Beltane culminates with the crowning of the Beltane Queen on the steps in front of the parish church. The queen and her court are chosen from one of the three primary schools in the town. The adult principal of the festival is the Cornet, a local young man chosen by the committee as being worthy of representing the town. He carries the town standard for a year.

Beltane is a festival that once marked the return of summer with the lighting of fires where people could burn their bedding and floor coverings used throughout the winter. The **Common Riding** occurs every year in June or July in most of the Border towns. The Borderers pay their respects to

Neidpath Castle

those who in the past risked their lives by protecting the townspeople from adjoining landowners or reivers who might have encroached upon the Common Lands of the town. The townspeople ride out around the boundaries with much ceremony.

Neidpath Castle is a tall 14th century tower house, which stands high above the River Tweed. It seems wonderfully mysterious and dramatic when viewed through the trees and shrubby vegetation as you walk the footpath beside the wide river. The tower is reputed to be haunted by Jean Douglas, the subject of Sir Walter Scott's tragic poem 'The Maid of Neidpath'.

1 Turn right out of the car park and walk Chambers Terrace towards a fine oak in the middle of a tiny roundabout, planted in 1902 as a memorial of the coronation of King Edward VII. Go on across the road, with great care, and walk up a tree-lined ginnel, the John Buchan Way (JBW), the sign-post obscured by a bush. Continue up the tarmacked track and turn right to walk a narrow lane. Turn left as signed, at the end, and carry on up a narrow path beside school playing fields. Turn right at the end onto Craigerne Road and walk on below forest trees. Turn left at a T-jumction on the JBW and climb the slope to take a signed metal gate, on the right, beside the gates of Tantah House.

Walk 22

2 Beyond, follow the distinct grassy track to a gate and then climb steadily right up a green trod. Pause here and look down on Peebles and its fine Hydro set below a wooded slope, with the Glentress hills behind. At the Y-junction, below overhead power lines, take the left branch and ascend to a waymark. Carry on the wide grassy trod ignoring a vehicle track climbing a hill to the left. Stroll on the pleasing track that leads you past the Red Well to an ancient settlement on Cademuir Hill, which you will want to explore.

3 At this point the JBW bears left (waymarked) and goes downhill towards the road. This walk continues winding to the right and beginning the climb, on a grassy trod, towards the summit of the hill. As you near the top, take a narrow path left to a tiny circle of rocks marking the highest point on the ridge, 1300ft/400m. This is also the site of the largest of two fortified settlements, built between the late BC and the 1st century AD. Return down the short narrow path to join the grassy trod and continue, left, along the ridge. Just before the site of the second fort, look for many spikey rocks firmly embedded in the ground. They are called chevaux de frise (Horses of Frisia) and were intended to disrupt charging attackers. Beyond lies a vast expanse of stone, the remains of a huge enclosing wall that once encircled this fine strategic point. It is believed that the two forts might have been abandoned around the arrival of the Romans in 80AD.

4 After clambering up through the low bank of stone and wandering around the site, stand by the sturdy cairn to enjoy the spectacular views. Then return over the ruined wall at the same place and turn left down a good grassy swathe. At a cross of tracks, turn left and descend a steepish section, still on a good trod. Curve right and go down, more gently, to pass to the right of a circular sheepfold. Continue down the slopes to cross a wide track as you near a wall and then bear left to join a narrow road (JBW). Turn right and soon wind right to walk along the flood bank of the pretty Manor Water, overhung with alders and small leaved lime. At the three picnic tables you might wish to stop for a break in this idyllic corner of the Borders. From here you might spot nesting lapwings seeing off a hungry kestrel.

5 Walk on along the road and cross the road bridge over the burn. Wind right with the road and at a junction keep right to pass the few houses and the church at Kirkton Manor. Just beyond the church turn left through access gates and stroll on along an unmade track lined with wild flowers in the summer and overhung by

Kestrel

trees. Continue for ½ mile/1km until you reach a signpost on the left, directing you, right, towards the River Tweed. Go through a gate and walk a glorious grassy track gently descending to a gate giving access to a fine path along the side of the river, which flows sedately to your left. Here grow wood cranesbill and water avens. Look for common sandpiper, heron and dipper as you go. The lovely path brings you to the splendid Manor Bridge, built in 1883.

6 Climb steps beside it to join the road and turn left to cross to the opposite side of the Tweed to take a kissing gate, on the right, to a path which leads up onto the disused railway track of the old Caledonian railway, which connected Peebles with Edinburgh, Glasgow and Carlisle. The track in summer is lined with dog rose, wild rose and innumerable other flowers. After a short distance, take a farm gate on the right and follow a narrow path that leads down to the side of the river once more. Enjoy this quiet way through meadows colourful with flowers to reach the fine skew viaduct that once carried the trains high above the river.

7 Head on beside the Tweed and then climb a little to a gate into woodland high above the river. The path rises and falls and is sometimes narrow and strewn with roots. Go on to pass Neidpath Castle and continue round a huge bend to find a good place from where to photograph the romantic castle. Then walk on soon to reach vast Hay Lodge Park. Continue beside the river, where on the weir, you might spot a fine family of goosanders. Then just before Tweed Bridge, wind left to reach a road. Turn right and right again to cross the bridge and then left to return to the car park.

Meadow Cranesbill

Practicals

Type of walk: *Good grassy tracks and paths. Superb views. Some exciting ancient sites high up on the Cademuir Hills and a long floriferous walk along the side of the mighty Tweed.*

Total distance: 10 miles/16.5km

Time: 4–5 hours

Maps: OS Explorer 337/Landranger 73

Innerleithen and Walkerburn

Park by the Leithen Water, grid ref 333369. Access this by Leithen Road, which leads north off the A72, just before the road bridge over the burn. The actual car park is signed but not the turn to it.

Both **Innerleithen and Walkerburn**, visited on this walk, were busy textile towns in the Tweed valley. The first custom designed woollen mill was built in Innerleithen in 1788. In the 1960s and 70s the woollen industry declined but Innerleithen is still famous for its splendid cashmere.

Cuddy Brig, built in 1701, is a stone built arch across the Leithen Water and is crossed on this walk. Here you might spot a dipper bobbing on the stones around which swirl the hurrying water. Continuing left

Cuddy Brig, Innerleithen

along the Leithen Water you reach Jenny's stepping stones that lead across the Leithen Water to Jenny's well, named after Jenny Baptie who sold home-made sweets from her cottage just across the road from the well.

1   Walk on along the road from the car park and, very soon, pass a house, next to the burn, with a splendid garden. Just beyond, turn right along a wide ginnel, signed to Pirn Hill. Cross the superb Cuddy Brig and turn left to walk along the side of the burn to take the stepping stones across to see Jenny's Well. Return to the

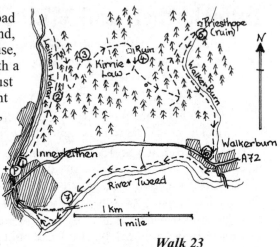

Walk 23

lovely bridge and climb steps, to a higher track, where you walk left. Listen for nuthatches and blackcaps as you continue along the track lined with deciduous trees and lush bushes. The track then leads into a conifer plantation, with a steep drop down to the valley and trees climbing very steeply to the right, the good track continuing easily.

2   Then the conifers end on the left and a fenced path carries on above Innerleithen golf course, with the plantation rearing up to the right. When just before the access track to the clubhouse of the course, well below, take the signposted 'Walkerburn and Priesthope' wide track slanting up sharp right into the plantation. Ignore any left or right turns made by mountain bikers (though this isn't an official cyclist's track) and after ½ mile/1km, take a waymarked narrower track climbing steadily and follow it as it makes a wide swing left to continue through a very dark part of the forest. The way narrows a little and goes on climbing relentlessly for ¾ mile/1.4km.

3   Suddenly there is light at the end of the 'tunnel' as the path climbs on up, with a vast area of clearfell to the left and conifers to the right. Pause here to look down on the valley, far below, where you can see part of the golf course. Cross a large parking area for forest vehicles

84

and then the forest road. Go on up into more conifers that soon form an arch overhead though some low branches have been cut. And then after ¼ mile/0.5km you reach the edge of the trees and the track takes you over heather moorland, climbing steadily, to come upon a monstrous disused walled reservoir now empty and left to decay. Unfortunately the high walls have provided a blackboard for spray painters to add their comments.

4 Wind round to the right on the track, with the disused building to your right and continue on up through the heather on a pleasing track. A short way along a narrower path leads off left, which you take. This soon begins a steepish descent towards more conifers, passing an old pumping station to the right and a large pipe, covered in moss, leading from it into the trees. Carry on into the forest to start a long steep descent on a needle-littered path. Half way down pass through a tiny green oasis and go on to descend another steep drop through the tightly packed trees to a T-junction where you turn left. Notice as you go the mass of oak fern on the right side of the track and a profusion of foxgloves relieving the rather gloomy way. The track, after just over a mile, reaches Priesthope, another oasis of green, this one larger. On the left, beyond a farm gate, stands a ruined croft, and sheep and their lambs graze peacefully.

5 Turn right here to walk along a wider track, with heather edging the sides and a variety of coniferous trees on either side, to reach a gate out onto grassy slopes. Follow the pleasing continuing grassy trod winding round the hillside, with the very narrow Walker Burn down to your left. As you near the narrow edge of a plantation on the right, look for a waymarked small gate on the left. Then a recently constructed path descends through more gates beside the burn, where grow clumps of the delightful orange monkey flower. Follow the path downhill to reach some farm outbuildings. Cross a track to go through a gate and wind left round more buildings to reach the A72 at the village of Walkerburn.

6 Cross the A-road with care and go on along Caberston Road. Where the road turns left, go through a farm gate to the side of the River Tweed and walk right, with the lovely wide river to your left. Continue along the riverside path enjoying the innumerable sand martins, skimming the water's surface for food for their young in the plethora of holes in the riverbank.

Sand Martins

Look right to see the houses of the village, many of them built for the workers at the woollen mill. Soon you need to take a gate on the right to wind round a house on the riverbank and then return to the waterside beyond.

7 Carry on along the riverbank to pass under the disused railway bridge. If the river is very high, turn right and walk the disused railway track into Innerleithen. If not carry on until just before a gate on the riverside and turn right to walk beside a fence, on the right, into the village. Some walkers still with energy left might wish to go through the small gate and find their way to a large pebbly area where the Leithen Water joins the Tweed. Here among the pebbles thrive masses of the glorious viper's bugloss, a deep purple-violet coloured flower. Wind round right on a little path, parallel with the Leithen, to a gate and walk ahead to join the earlier path, last described, where you turn left to walk a rough track to reach the houses of the village. Continue up the road to turn left onto the A-road. Cross the road bridge over the Leithen Water, then the main road by the bollard to walk up Leithen Road to reach the parking area.

Viper's Bugloss

Practicals

Type of walk: *Good tracks and paths through the immense conifer forest provide good walking for a wet and windy day though some of the paths are steep. The return along the side of the Tweed is a delight.*

Total distance: 8½ miles/13.5km
Time: 4–5 hours
Maps: OS Explorer 337/Landranger 73

Walk 24

Yair and Neidpath Hill

Park in the forestry car park at Yair Bridge, grid ref 459325. To access this, take the A707 from Selkirk towards Peebles. The car park is on the left just before the bridge over the Tweed.

Ashiestiel Bridge, which was an early crossing of the Tweed, is an amazing single arch, built of whinstone rubble in 1847. During its original construction it collapsed before the arch was completed. It spans 132ft/41m and it measures 203ft/63m in length, which includes its approaches. Its structure was repaired in 1952.

1 Turn left along the A707 and cross Yair Bridge over the Tweed. It is a narrow bridge controlled by traffic lights, but there are refuges along it. At the far end bear left, still on the A707, for 55yds/50m and then follow the 'Southern Upland Way' (SUW) and 'footpath to Galashiels' sign on the

Ashiestiel Bridge

right to walk **Walk 24**
between farm
buildings and
into a wood.
The wood is
mainly beech
with a carpet of bluebells
and wood anemones in spring.
Chiffchaffs and blackcaps sing
from the bushes and siskins indulge
in song flights above the trees. Cross
an estate drive to Fairnilee House and
carry on up the SUW between fields.
Enter a shelter belt of Scots pine and
bear right through the trees. Beyond,
descend slightly, ignoring a track on the
left, then climb again to go through a gate
and turn left, leaving the SUW to follow a sign
for Galashields Circuit. Contour below a wood and then head slightly
uphill, going past two large heaps of stones, probably field clearance,
to pass through a gate. Climb the next field, past more stone heaps,
heading for a shallow valley leading up towards the top of Neidpath
Hill. Wind right and then left to a gate in the wall on the ridge. Beyond,
turn left for the short walk to the cairn. The view from here is splendid.

2   Return to the gate and walk on with the wall to your right. At a steep
    slope in front of you, take any of the several paths; they all rejoin
    beyond the hill. Carry on along the line of the wall and follow it right
    round beside a plantation and down the other side of the heathery
    field to go through a wicket gate to a signpost. Beyond, turn left to
    follow the wall, now on your left, downhill. After the next gate, keep
    left down by the burn. Pass through the next gate and follow a clear,
    steadily improving track that runs along the hillside through gorse
    bushes, magnificent in spring. The path goes on into woodland beside
    the Blakehope Burn and down through the attractive glen. At the foot
    of the glen it swings right above the wall of the church and graveyard.
    Carry on the grassy path, above a garden wall, until you reach a sign-
    post indicating a left turn downhill. This is quite steep but has rails in
    the steepest places. Soon you are down at the road in Caddonfoot.

3   Cross the main road with care and walk over the footbridge beside
    the road bridge. Turn left immediately to walk down a metalled road
    towards the Tweed. Where it stops carry on the small footpath along

the riverbank. At the start of a large field take the stile into it and walk with care along the edge, just inside the fence. It is possible to get along the riverbank before the vegetation gets too high but it is very rough and difficult in places. At the end of the field go through a hurdle gate and continue along the now distinct footpath through pleasant woodland, with primroses on the bank to your right, to climb steps to a stile onto the road. Turn left and cross Ashiestiel Bridge over the Tweed.

4 Walk on along the road for 110yds/100m and turn left into a forest track, signed Peel Path to Yair. This is a reinforced track that is a cycle path as well as a walking way. Take the first left turn towards the river and enjoy the open views. Soon the track winds right into conifers but a small path continues along the riverbank, opposite Caddonfoot. Listen for common sandpipers and look for them bobbing on the rocks. At a wall the riverside path ends. Climb steps up to the track and continue along between fields. It then runs into the beautiful mature woodlands around Yair House and begins to descend, winding right with a wall to the left and then a walled garden to the right. Turn left, go past Yair Farm and keep left. The track becomes a metalled road running along by the Tweed to Yair Bridge, where you join the A707 and return to the car park.

Common Sandpiper

Practicals

Type of walk: *Very satisfactory, mainly on good paths, and well-waymarked.*

Total distance: 7 miles/11.4km
Time: 4 hours
Maps: OS Explorer 338/Landranger 73

Walk 25

The Eildon Hills, Trimontium and Leaderfoot Viaduct

Park in Melrose, in the car park by the Abbey, grid reference 547342 (free from October to April but there is a charge in summer). If this car park is full there are various others in Melrose.

For part of this walk, the route follows the excellently arrowed **St Cuthbert's Way**, the long distance path that starts at Melrose. It was in this attractive town, around 650AD, that the saint is believed to have started his monastic life. Eventually he went to Lindisfarne as Prior and became well known for his healing powers. Then he was appointed Bishop of Lindisfarne.

The ruined 12th century Melrose Abbey is the burial place of the casket believed to contain the heart of **Robert the Bruce**.

Thomas the Rhymer was a 13th century Scottish laird and reputed prophet. Popular esteem of Thomas lived on for centuries after his death and for many years his supernatural powers rivalled those of Merlin.

St Cuthbert's Way is 62½ miles long and was opened in 1996. The route climbs through the fine triple-topped **Eildon Hills** of which the 18th century poet Andrew Scott of Bowden wrote:

Leaderfoot Viaduct

O Eildon Hills,
  Huge sisters three,
As fair you rise as any.
Scotia has higher hills
  than thee,
But few gleam half as
  bonny.

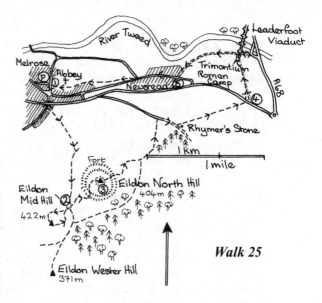

Walk 25

1 Leave the car park in Melrose to walk up Abbey Street to the Market Square. Cross and walk ahead up past the Station Hotel and on under the Melrose bypass. A short distance up the hill there is a ginnel on the left between houses, signed for St. Cuthbert's Way and the Eildon Walk, with steps leading down to a bridge and then a long flight of wooden steps up the hillside. There are seats at intervals as you climb. Go through a gate at the top of the steps and on up a waymarked fenced path. Cross a track and continue to the next kissing gate. Beyond this the path turns right and heads for the col between the two highest hills, climbing gently through gorse which is magnificent in spring. As you approach the col you come into heather and should see and hear red grouse.

2 Turn right at the col towards Mid Hill (1366ft), which is the highest of the three. Ignore paths going off to the sides. Two paths can be seen climbing the hill; go up one and down the other. The left one is a little steeper. On the summit stands a trig point and a view indicator, and there is a splendid view on a clear day. Return to the col and climb straight ahead up Eildon North Hill (1313ft). Where the path divides you can take either branch as they join again higher up, but the right branch is a lovely grassy zigzag with a very easy gradient. It curls round to the summit, where you can see the shape of the base of the old Roman signal station, and banks of the fortifications.

3 Walk ahead from the summit and down the steep grassy path on the far side of the hill. This is still waymarked with the three hills symbol of the Eildon Walk. At the foot of the hill, the path, wet in places, winds down through gorse to a kissing gate and then down an ash-lined way beside a small burn to a metalled road. Turn right. The road is closed to traffic except for access. Go round the barrier and on to the Rhymer's Stone, and the viewpoint over the valley. Turn left here, off the road, to follow a grassy track between hedges. Ignore a branch to the left and walk ahead beside an old beech hedge, now a row of trees, then through fields to reach the main road. There is a clear view in both directions but the traffic moves very fast so cross with great care.

4   Go through a gate beside a large sign for Broomhill, and go straight ahead where the main track bends right. About 22yds/20m further on, bear left onto an old railway line and follow the path along it through a deep cutting spanned by a fine bridge, then out into fields. On the left is a board telling details of the Roman camp of Trimontium, which used to occupy the field in front. There is a mock-up of a signal tower to the right. Cross the stile by the board and go down the edge of the field to a gate with steps down to a road; this one also is closed to vehicles. The magnificent Leaderfoot Viaduct is directly in front of you here, soaring over the Tweed. If you want a better view of it turn right and walk down to the old road bridge, which is also splendid. Then return up the old road and walk along it to the village of Newstead. At frequent intervals along the roadside there are boards telling about the Roman camps and associated buildings, and a memorial stone. It is a pity that there is so little to see on the ground.

5   In Newstead turn right at the road and walk downhill through the attractive village. Bend left and turn left where there is a road sign for Melrose pointing right. A few steps along the road take the waymarked path on the right, called the Prior's Walk. This runs below houses and then along a bank. It comes to a housing development; keep right and soon the path resumes, bringing you back along the edge of the Abbey grounds and into Melrose beside the car park.

Red Grouse

Practicals

Type of walk: *A glorious hill climb.*

Total distance: 6½ miles/10.6km
Time: 3–4 hours
Maps: OS Explorer 338/Landranger 73

Walk 26

Dryburgh Abbey and the River Tweed

Park opposite the entrance to Dryburgh Abbey, grid ref 593317. To access this, turn east off the A68 to drive through St Boswells on the B6404. After crossing the Tweed, turn left along the B6356 and follow the signs to Dryburgh.

The gracious, sandstone ruins of **Dryburgh Abbey** nestle in a huge loop of the River Tweed. The white canons chose this idyllic spot, in 1150, as a refuge for those who, weary of this life, wanted to prepare for the next. Alas, the passing armies of the English made sure this glorious peace did not last and by 1544 the abbey was in ruins, never to recover.

An **intriguing legend** tells of a landowner who buried his wife in the abbey grounds; she had been interred with her wedding ring. That night the sexton dug up the

Dryburgh Abbey

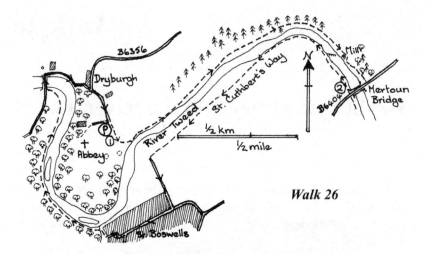

Walk 26

coffin and tried to cut off her finger. However, the wife was not dead and when she sat up, the terrified thief fled. She returned to her family house and knocked on the door. Her husband said to his family that if his wife had still been alive, that was her knock. What happened next – we don't know.

Through all the turmoil at the abbey, the **River Tweed** has flowed serenely by. It rises in the Tweedsmuir Hills and after 97 miles reaches the sea at Berwick. It is a salmon river and its prolific autumn run was first recorded and harvested by the monks.

1 Walk on from the parking area, with the toilets to your left and the grounds of the abbey to the right. After 100yds/92m take a signposted stile, left, and follow the pleasing way that keeps parallel with the Tweed, sometimes high above it and sometimes beside the water where you might spot a kingfisher. Once round the huge curve in the Tweed, take the stile in the fence on your right to descend to the river's edge. Here anglers wade in the shallow water. Continue to Mertoun Bridge, a narrow road bridge, which you should cross with care. At its end go down steps, on the right, to return along the bank of the bonny river, walking St Cuthbert's Way, the long distance footpath from Melrose to Lindisfarne.

2 Follow the waymarked route and then take the metalled left turn to pass St Boswells' Golf Clubhouse. Continue on to St Boswells where you turn right. After dawdling through the delightful village, turn right again as directed by the signpost, just before the extensive green ahead. At the end of short Hamilton Place, turn right and follow the

waymarked path to continue beside the Tweed. This brings you to a fine suspension bridge over the wide river, with a dramatic gazebo on a hillock beyond. Once across, turn right and continue to the T-junction. Go right again to return to the abbey, with time left to enjoy the superb ruins.

Salmon

CMI

Practicals

Type of walk: *This is a grand walk along the banks of the lovely River Tweed, a peaceful way once steeped in violence.*

Total distance: 4 miles/6.5km
Time: 2–3 hours
Maps: OS Explorer 338/Landranger 74

Walk 27

River Teviot from Kelso

Park in the free car park behind Kelso Abbey, grid ref 729338.

Kelso is a largely agricultural community and hosts agricultural shows, steeple chasing at the famous racecourse and the Scottish Championship Dog Show.

The **12th century Kelso Abbey** suffered in the Border wars and was mostly destroyed in September 1545 by the Earl of Hertford. Since the Reformation in Scotland followed in 1560 there was no time to rebuild the abbey. It was used as a parish church until 1805 but then fell into disrepair.

Roxburgh Castle, once the most important castle in Scotland, was built by King David I in the 12th century. He worked hard to bring trade and modern forms of government to Scotland. The castle was well placed to defend prosperous Kelso and lands about the Border, but it was not enough. It changed hands ten times over the next 400 years and was finally razed to the ground by the wife of James II in

Kelso Abbey

revenge for his death which occurred while he was successfully be-sieging the castle.

The five-arched bridge spanning the Tweed was the model for London's Waterloo Bridge.

Floors Castle can be seen from this walk. It is Scotland's largest inhabited castle and the home of the Duke and Duchess of Roxburgh.

1 After visiting the ruins of the Abbey, leave by the gates and turn left to go past the war memorial in its magnificent flower garden. Cross the very long Rennie Bridge over the River Tweed and read the plaque at its end, which tells you about its lights. Turn right onto the A699 and walk beside the wide surging Tweed to where it is joined by the Teviot. Cross the road and carry on along the pavement to wind round right to go over the Teviot Bridge, with care. This is another splendid bridge, much more ornate than Rennie's. It has virtually no pavement but it does have several escape recesses so use one of these to see the fine river below. Walk on along the pavement, go past several dwellings and, a short way beyond, pass through a stone step stile on the left and down steps to the riverbank and walk upstream, on the Borders Abbeys Way.

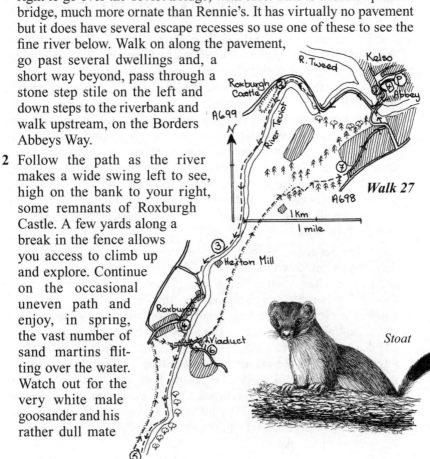

2 Follow the path as the river makes a wide swing left to see, high on the bank to your right, some remnants of Roxburgh Castle. A few yards along a break in the fence allows you access to climb up and explore. Continue on the occasional uneven path and enjoy, in spring, the vast number of sand martins flit-ting over the water. Watch out for the very white male goosander and his rather dull mate

Walk 27

Stoat

her drabness relieved by her bright red-brown head. You will also see many mallards and pairs of swans on the water. In the bushes and trees that occasionally grow beside the water, look for goldfinch, long-tailed tit, reed bunting and yellowhammer.

3   Then the path moves out into more open countryside, with arable crops to the right and the stately river flowing to your left. Soon you reach a hedge stretching down the field to your right and almost to the river-bank. Here climb a stile and move right to pass through a waymarked gate to join a wide grassy trod, with the fence to your left. Across the river stands the attractive Heiton Mill. Walk on round the field, with a thick thorn hedge to your left. Continue on, now high above the Teviot. At the next fence, wind round the corner of a huge field to take a way-marked step stile onto a narrow hedged lane and turn left. Walk on through the outbuildings of Roxburgh Mill and on towards Roxburgh village.

4   Before the road winds right, follow the sign for the Borders Abbeys Way and turn down left on a rough track and then turn left again. There is a superb view of the viaduct spanning the river. Carry on down the lane to reach the side of the Teviot. Pass under the viaduct and stroll on beside the river on a track. A good path goes on with a ruined mill on the opposite bank. This is a lovely section of the Teviot. Pass through a kissing gate and make your way over rough ground, choosing the easiest of several paths. Soon a good path goes on until you reach a boundary wall. Turn right, ignoring the continuing path along the riv-erbank. Climb up the pasture to a very obvious huge ladder that leads up to the defunct Kelso – Jedburgh railway line. (If the steps prove too daunting, walk right up the slope to a gate onto the track, a short way along.) Turn right.

5   Stride the hedged level track for just over a mile, with the occasional delightful view down on the river. You might also see roe deer, jays and a stoat. Then when the track ends, descend a path to the road, just outside Roxburgh. Turn right and take, immediately right, a gate onto another stretch of old railway track. Follow this high above the sur-rounding fields until you near the gates that bar entry to the viaduct, and descend right on a steep rough track to arrive at the foot of the huge pillars supporting the viaduct. Cross the long footbridge, each section fixed to a viaduct pillar over the Teviot. Follow the path beyond to a minor road, turn right and go under a viaduct arch and follow the road as it swings round left for 220yds/200m. As you climb, look over the wall and into the woodland where vast numbers of white violets carpet the ground in late April.

6 At a bend in the road, take the signed left turn to walk a track. Go past an old siding, it too covered in white violets, and then turn right to continue on the disused railway track. This is good underfoot to begin with but it does become muddy and very wet in places. It continues on this way for 1 ½ miles/2.4km but there is always a narrow dry patch to get round the water though one large pool might create a problem. As you stride on

White Violets

look left across the valley to see the huge Floors Castle. Very soon you come level with a large white house to the right. Here descend a path to take the waymarked gate on the right. Turn left and walk a wide track, with young woodland to your right and the now very overgrown railway line over the fence to your left. Wind round right at the fence ahead and, half way up the slope, take a gate on the left. Stride a narrow path through an arable crop to a gate opposite. Turn right and walk a track, also good at first, but it does become deeply puddled at times, before it reaches a road.

7 Cross with care and walk left, downhill, until you reach a junction near a garage. Cross this road with care and descend left to the Millennium viewpoint where you will want to pause. Then descend steps to the right of the viewpoint, cross the attractive park and climb steps to the Rennie Bridge. Walk right and continue on to where you have parked.

Practicals

Type of walk: *The riverside path is a delight for all the way. The return on the railway track has many pleasing parts but also some very wet areas that you have to edge round. The views, the peace and the wildlife are magic. After continuous rain you might wish to avoid the return along the railway track by returning beside the river – unless of course it has overflowed its banks – perhaps choose another day.*

Total distance: 9 miles/14.5km

Time: 4–5 hours

Maps: OS Explorers 339 and OL16/Landranger 74

Walk 28

Coldstream

Park in Coldstream's Home Park car park beside the Castle Hotel, grid ref 841397. Access the village from the west by the A698 or from the north-east by the A6112.

The **village of Coldstream** lies on the north bank of the River Tweed, which here forms the boundary between Scotland and England. Its history is linked with the Coldstream Guards who were formed in1650, and with the battle of Flodden Field.

The **Hirsel** is the ancestral home of the Douglas Home family. A network of paths through the lovely grounds is a joy to walk.

The **water banks**, strolled along at the start of the walk, beside the River Leet and the River Tweed, were constructed in 1820 by prisoners from the 1815 Napoleonic wars at the behest of Sir James Majoriebanks. When in winter the land is flooded the water brings down rich loam for growing arable crops.

Visitor Centre, the Hirsel estate

1 From the car park, cross the road and walk right down Main Street to go over the bridge across the River Leet. At the bridge end, turn left and where the road divides take the right branch. Soon the houses cease and a track goes left over a footbridge across the old mill leat. At the information panel, follow the concrete track ahead over a large arable field, with the Leet to your left. Ignore the right turn and keep ahead parallel with the river, which is lined with trees on the far bank. Continue along the flood bank to reach the junction of the Leet with the River Tweed, the latter hurrying on its way below Coldstream, the small linear village that sits high above. Here you might spot heron, mallard and goosander.

2 Bear right here along the floodbank, where the Tweed, on your left, makes a very wide curve. Beyond lies England. Continue on a good path, past a weir and then on, keeping to the riverside of Lees fishing bothy, where you might spot anglers hoping to catch a splendid salmon for which the Tweed is famous. Stroll the lovely way now through beech woodland, still beside the river, to pass the towered Lees House. Follow the waymarks that direct you into an arable field and carry on close beside the river and then on along a lengthy stretch of turf, delightful to walk on, past several small islands in the river beside you. Very soon after you reach a large island, which divides the river, you reach a gate and a stile to Fireburnmill. Beyond, walk uphill to pass cottages on the left and a house on the right, to come to a road junction, where the A698 and A697 join. Cross with care to the far side of the A697.

3 Take a few steps up the A697, signposted to Edinburgh, to turn right into deciduous woodland as directed by a waymarked post. At the top of the slope, join a track and turn left to continue through the lovely trees of Dundock Wood. Ignore a signed track, left, and go ahead towards Hirsel Lake. At the T-junction turn right, with forest trees to the left, through which you have glimpses of the lake. As you near the Visitor Centre in the old farm steading, part of the Hirsel Estate, you might wish to visit the museum and tearoom if they are open. The

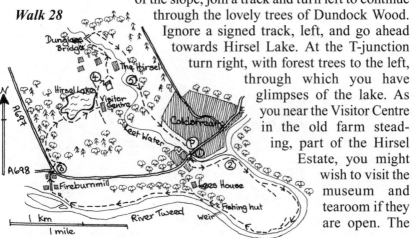

Walk 28

track winds left in front of the buildings and there are large seats at the water's edge from which to enjoy the bird life on the charming reed–fringed lake.

4 Carry on along the track and bear right at a Y-junction, following the red arrows to pass behind The Hirsel House, with its Ha Ha. Continue on the track to go by a cow arch, on the right, where at one time cattle were brought under the driveway to the dairy, out of sight of the big house. Stroll on through the extensive grounds. Bear right to pass two red waymarks, one after the other. Take the second one, which directs you off the main track and down into the fine deciduous woodland to walk beside the Leet Water. Then cross the Dunglass Bridge over the burn. Climb steps and take the delightful red waymarked path, right, through more woodland, returning along the opposite side of the Leet. From here you have another view of The Hirsel to your right.

Dabchick

5 Wind round left on another well waymarked track, lined in early spring with snowdrops, which brings you close to the Leet again. Then curve left, with the track following yellow way-marks and at a division keep to the left branch. Carry on soon to stroll a small tree-lined path through a narrow shallow valley. Follow this path all the way until you reach a gate into the car park.

Practicals

Type of walk: *Pleasing tracks, grassy trods, and narrow paths, all quite delightful.*

Distance: 6 miles/9.5km

Time: 3–4 hours

Maps: OS Explorer 339/Landranger 74

Walk 29

White Law and Halterburn
(near Kirk Yetholm)

Park in the large grassy space between the road and the burn at Halterburn, grid ref 840277, shortly after crossing the cattle grid. To access this, drive south on a minor road from the village green in Kirk Yetholm, following signs for Halterburn and also the Pennine Way.

The Pennine Way (PW) runs for 268 miles along Britain's spine. It starts at Edale, the plague village in Derbyshire, and continues to Kirk Yetholm, just inside the Scottish border. It is a tough wild route and stays that way from start to finish crossing much glorious hill country. In 1935 Tom Stephenson, a member of the Ramblers' Association, wrote an article for the Daily Herald raising the idea of a long distance trail, one similar to North America's John Muir Trail through the Rockies. On the 24th April 1965 the Pennine Way was officially opened and Tom Stephenson realised his long-held dream when he was present with more than 2,000 people gathered on Malham Moor to celebrate.

The Stob Stones

1 Leave the car park following the sign for the PW and St. Cuthbert's Way. Cross a wooden bridge over the Halter Burn and walk uphill with the wall to your left on a grassy path. At the top of the wall a steeper path goes straight ahead up the slopes of Green Humbleton, 943ft/287m, which has the ring walls of an ancient fort on top. However, if you do not want such a steep climb, the main PW winds, right, around the side of the hill and ascends more gently to the col on the far side. Bear right and follow the path up the ridge to a sign-post, where the St. Cuthbert's Way goes left. Carry on along the PW. Soon you reach a Y-junction, where the better-used path is the left branch, but the right one takes you past two standing stones, the Stob Stones. Look for wheatears flitting about the stones and along the walls as you continue. The paths rejoin at a wall and a stile. Do not go through into England.

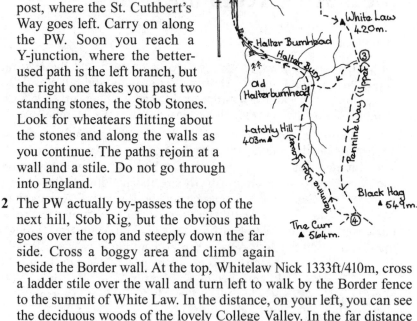

Walk 29

2 The PW actually by-passes the top of the next hill, Stob Rig, but the obvious path goes over the top and steeply down the far side. Cross a boggy area and climb again beside the Border wall. At the top, Whitelaw Nick 1333ft/410m, cross a ladder stile over the wall and turn left to walk by the Border fence to the summit of White Law. In the distance, on your left, you can see the deciduous woods of the lovely College Valley. In the far distance is the sea. To the right are endless rounded Cheviots and, behind all, the Tweed valley with the Eildons standing proud in the centre.

3 Wind right again and go downhill to a Border gate, which you ignore. If the weather has changed and you need to cut the walk short, turn right and take a narrow trod which soon becomes a clear path winding round the valley side. It becomes rather divided, but head for a ruin in a clump of trees, cross the burn and join the track downhill. To continue the main walk climb gently by the fence from the gate along a rounded ridge called Steer Rig. After 1 mile/1.5km pass through a gate. Carry on up to the top where, suddenly, you can see the great whaleback of Cheviot ahead, with the Schil's stony summit to its right and the long ridge round to Windy Gyle beyond. Go through another gate, then head away from the Border fence and go downhill to a signpost.

4 Here turn sharply right, signed 'Pennine Way Low Level Route', and descend gently along the hillside, through a gate and on down a long winding descent. Go though another gate in the wall to your right and carry on along the grassy way. Soon the ruins of Old Halterburnhead come into view, surrounded by ash and sycamore - the short cut from the upper path is clearly visible, and joins it near here. Go on down with the track, which becomes more stony. Look out for a signpost, shortly before the gate across the track at Halterburnhead Farm, which directs you right, down to the burn. Cross on a footbridge and climb the opposite slope to a gate. Beyond, follow the wall to your left to reach another gate and steps down to a fenced way through a field to join a reinforced track. Turn right and pass sheds on the right. Go through the small gate to the right of a cattle grid and walk down the metalled road for 1 mile/1.5km past the tiny settlement of Halterburn and back to your car.

Wheatear

Practicals

Type of walk: *Very pleasant, well-signed way along the Border fence. The climbs are quite gentle although it does go up and down more than one might expect.*

Total distance: 7 miles/11.5km
Time: 4 hours
Maps: OS Explorer OL 16/Landranger 74

Walk 30

Windy Gyle

Park at Cocklawfoot, in a large space on the left where the metalled road ends and a track goes off on the right to Kelsocleuch, grid ref 852186. Do not block the farmer's turning space. To access this, turn south off the B6401 one mile south of Town Yetholm, onto a minor road signed to Cocklawfoot, 7 miles (11.4km). Keep right at two junctions and cross the ford on the River Bowmont, or if too deep, there is a bridge on a loop of track as an alternative.

Clennell Street is an old drove road, used for moving cattle from one side of the border to the other, both legally by drovers and illegally by reivers. The crossing on this walk was known as Hexpathgate, and in the 15th and 16th centuries was a meeting point for the Border wardens, who were responsible for keeping the peace, and to discuss terms.

Russell's Cairn on **Windy Gyle** 1983ft/610m is a Bronze Age burial cairn. It was named in memory of the English Lord Francis Russell, who was shot and killed at a meeting under truce on the summit of Windy Gyle in 1585.

Russell's Cairn, Windy Gyle

1 Walk on along the track towards Cocklawfoot Farm and either ford the river or go over the metal bridge. Listen for common sandpipers, and watch the house martins flying low over the water. Go through a gate into the wide farmyard and head right to a gate with a signpost

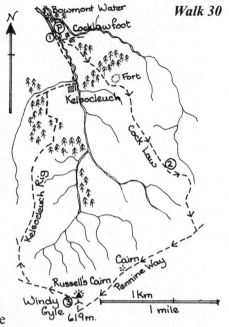

under a large tree. The sign is to Alwinton via Clennell Street. Go through the gate and climb the pleasant track up the large pasture beyond. Pass a wood on your left, and walk up to a gate into a plantation. The path continues through the trees and out at the far side onto open fell. It winds round the side of a hill with a fort on top and on up Cock Law, 1334ft/416m, with an ever widening view to Cheviot and Windy Gyle.

2 Descend slightly to a gate and then wind round a hill seamed with banks and ditches; someone was very busy here in the past. Walk on beside a fence to reach the Border, a gate and signpost for the Pennine Way (PW), which crosses Clennell Street here. Turn right to walk the PW. Purists who wish to remain in Scotland can cross a stile back and walk on the other side of the fence, but the ground is a combination of deep heather and wet peat hags. Most people will prefer to stay on the English side where the path is paved with stone flags over the wet areas and is very clear and easy all the way. Go through a gate. There is a large heap of stones on the right a little further on which is a Bronze Age burial cairn. Carry on up to the top of the ridge and go through a gate back into Scotland. Walk over to the large cairn and trig point at the summit of Windy Gyle. The cairn is another Bronze Age burial cairn, called Russell's Cairn.

3 Carry on along the PW as it descends Windy Rig, enjoying the views of Cheviot displaying the great gash in its flank called the Hen Hole. Near the col at the bottom the PW goes left through a gate but this walk goes on along the right side of the fence and up to another gate. Do not go through but bear right, contouring along the hillside and round onto a ridge, Kelsocleuch Rig. Walk down the lovely grassy path along the crest of the rig, through two gates, then on a smaller path to a gate into a felled plantation. Go on down the path to the bottom, and turn left onto a wide new forest track which runs around above the field wall.

Follow it round till it becomes a pleasant grassy way down by trees. Go through a gate at the bottom and turn right down a reinforced track towards the farm. Beyond it, turn left and follow the track along above the river to the car park.

Skylark

Practicals

Type of walk: *An easy pleasant ridge walk on good paths to a summit marked by its splendid cairn and excellent views of both the Borders and Northumberland. The English side of the Border is in the part of Northumberland used for exercises by the military and if the red flags are flying there may be soldiers around. However notices assure you that no live ammunition is ever used in the vicinity of the PW. The other possible restriction is that the farmer at Cocklawfoot has sheep lambing, usually in the first field above the farm, from 15th April to 15th May and would prefer you not to use this route then. Do not take dogs in the lambing season.*

Total distance: 6 miles/9.5km

Time: 3–4 hours

Maps: OS Explorer OL 16/Landranger 80

Walk 31

Grubbit Law and Kale Water

Park in the centre of Morebattle where there is plenty of roadside parking, grid ref 772249. To get to Morebattle take the B6401 which leaves the Hawick to Kelso road (A698) just south of Kalemouth, or the B6436 which runs south from Kelso.

Morebattle is a very old village. There was possibly a settlement here as early as the 7th century AD, although the present village originated in the reign of David 1st in the 12th century. In the year 1545 it was burnt by the Earl of Hertford acting on behalf of the English crown. He carried out a 'Rough Wooing' campaign in the Borders between 1544 and 1547, as part of a dispute with Mary, Queen of Scots. He also demolished all the four big abbeys in the region at this time.

Jubilee Bridge

Jubilee Bridge is an attractive cast iron footbridge over the Kale Water below Morebattle, which was built to commemorate Queen Victoria's Jubilee in 1887.

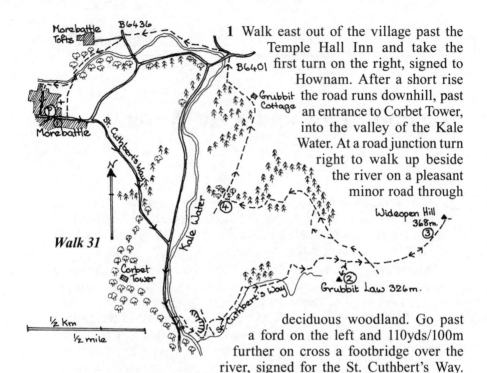

Walk 31

½ Km

½ mile

1 Walk east out of the village past the Temple Hall Inn and take the first turn on the right, signed to Hownam. After a short rise the road runs downhill, past an entrance to Corbet Tower, into the valley of the Kale Water. At a road junction turn right to walk up beside the river on a pleasant minor road through deciduous woodland. Go past a ford on the left and 110yds/100m further on cross a footbridge over the river, signed for the St. Cuthbert's Way. Cross the field ahead to join a track and turn right along it. It begins to climb, zigzagging up the hillside with a quarry to the left. Go over another track and continue climbing, winding round the hillside on a recently bulldozed track. Just before you reach a small plantation cross a ladder stile into the field on the right and walk up the grassy track beside the wood to a small gate at the top. Then follow the well-waymarked path as it winds up the hill ahead. Join a path coming in from the right and carry on round to a col. Turn right by the waymark and walk up to the top of Grubbit Law 988ft/326m, from where there is a splendid view.

2 Return to the col and walk right to a cross of paths. St. Cuthbert's Way goes straight on here; if the weather is good and you want to climb Wideopen Hill 1177ft/368m for another superb view follow the Way. Climb a stile over a wall and continue beside the wall to the top of the hill. This is the highest point on the St. Cuthbert's Way.

3 Retrace your steps to the path junction and turn right downhill, with a wall on your right. The path soon becomes a track and runs down to a field gate. Go through and either walk on along the track or follow the wall on your right down to a plantation; the two ways then rejoin.

Continue on the track as it winds down across the field towards another plantation and then beside it to a shed. Bear left between the plantation and a shelter belt of Scots pine, go through a gate and turn right to walk down by the pine trees. Look out for both grey and red-legged partridges in these fields. You could also see a stoat crossing the path.

4 Turn right to walk through the pines and cross a field on a good track. Walk past another plantation on the left then a cottage on the right, and on down to the Kale Water. The track soon reaches the road just to the right of a bridge. Cross the road but not the bridge and walk along a minor road opposite for a few steps. Here take a signed path through a gate on the left and walk along the riverbank, enjoying the swallows and sand martins that swoop over the water. The field narrows and then widens again; head away from the

river towards a small gate and signpost near the far corner. Cross the road beyond and bear left into the entrance track for Morebattle Tofts Farm. Almost immediately go through a gate into the field, on the left, which you cross to the riverbank. Take the gate in the far corner, and walk the lovely path through a wood, full of cherry blossom in spring, to cross the cast iron footbridge erected to commemorate the Jubilee of Queen Victoria. At the

Grey Partridges

far side, walk the path that continues along the riverside. It exits onto a lane where you turn left. Walk up into Morebattle and turn left at the main street to your car.

Practicals

Type of walk: *Mostly good paths and tracks. The part where the farmer has bulldozed the track is quite unpleasant at present but presumably it will settle down. The views from the top of Grubbit Law are splendid.*

Total distance: 4 miles/6.5km; extra ½ mile/1km if you climb Wideopen Hill.

Time: 2–3 hours

Maps: OS Explorer OL 16/Landranger 74

Walk 32

Waterloo Monument and Peniel Heugh

Park at Harestanes Countryside Visitor Centre, grid ref 642244. It is closed from October 31 to April 1 but the car park is open all the year round. Access this by the B6400 which crosses the A68 near Ancrum, north of Jedburgh.

The Waterloo Monument stands on the flattish top of Peniel Heugh, surrounded by rocky outcrops. It was erected by the 6th Marquis of Lothian, and his tenants, to celebrate Wellington's victory over Napoleon at the Battle of Waterloo. It stands 150ft/48m high, is constructed of whinstone from a local quarry and is topped with an attractive pagoda. The round tower can be seen for miles around and from the hill you have wonderful view of the lovely surrounding Border countryside.

1 From the car park walk back towards the road using a hedged and fenced footpath on the right side of the driveway. Follow the path into fine mixed woodland full of birdsong in the spring. Turn right to cross a footbridge over a stream that feeds into a pool and walk ahead to the signpost, where you turn left. Go on through more pleasing woodland to reach an estate road. Bear left, and go on to cross the B-road and head up a metalled track, towards 'Woodside, Gamekeepers House'. Before you reach the house, stroll right along a delightful track. In a few steps

Waterloo Monument, Peniel Heugh

bear right with Scots pine to the left and an arable field to the right. At the unclassified road, turn right and then left, to climb a rather rough track through huge forest trees. Ignore two right turns and continue steadily upwards.

2 Just before a gate out of the forest, you can see the monument on its hill. Ignore the gate, which is padlocked, and wind on, left, through the forest, passing through a small open area. Stroll on up with young trees deer-fenced to the left and with immature trees to the right until you can go through a gate. Beyond, carry on through the next gate, wind right and climb up beside a fence to reach the base of the monument. The views are superb. Look for Cheviot, Ettrick Forest, Teviotdale with triangular Rubers Law, the Eildon Hills, Tweedsmuir Hills and the Lammermuirs. After your long pause here, set off down beside the fence, on your left, once more, and through the two gates. Go on down to a junction of tracks.

3 Go straight ahead here (the right of two descending ahead) to drop down through the forest to join the unclassified road, at the right end of a stretch of wooden fencing. Cross the road and continue on to reach the track before Woodside Gamekeeper's Cottage. Turn right and 220ydds/200m along stroll a wide grassy track, left, through woodland beside a burn. When you reach the burn crossing, go left before it and continue on the lovely path, now part of St Cuthbert's Way, which descends gently, winding round the twists and turns of the little burn in its deep gill. As you go, in spring, listen for the calls of chiffchaff, blackcap and garden warbler. Where the path comes near to a steep slope down to the bridge over the gill, it is railed. All too soon you reach a small gate onto the B-road, which cross with care, to go through a similar gate. Walk ahead, go over the wooden bridge you crossed earlier, and walk on to the sign-post. Turn right and follow the path as it

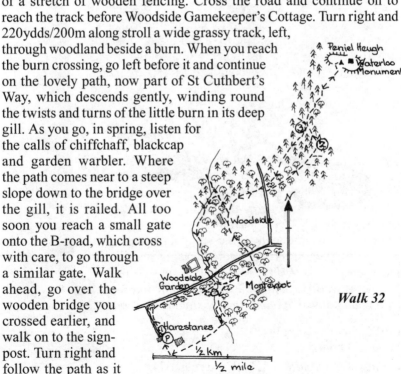

Walk 32

113

comes beside the little burn, where you might spot long tailed tit and nuthatch. A short way down descend steps to cross over the chuckling water. Beyond, turn left and drop down to an estate road. Stroll right on a narrow path beside the fence, with a magnificent avenue of forest trees to your left, to return to the car park.

Blackcap

Celandine

Practicals

Type of walk: *A delightful walk through fine deciduous woodland, on good paths that climb steadily to a wonderful viewpoint.*

Total distance: 4 miles/6.5km
Time: 2 hours
Maps: OS Explorer OL 16/Landranger 74

Walk 33

Bowhill and the Duchess's Drive

Park in the public car park at Bowhill House, grid ref 426279. Access this by turning left from the A708, 5km west of Selkirk at signs for Bowhill and follow more signs for the house. Fork right, before the house, for the car park. There maybe a charge for entry to the estate in summer.

Bowhill House is one of the homes of the Duke of Buccleugh and Queensberry. The present house dates from 1812, the building work accompanied by much formal planting and landscaping of the grounds.

Newark Castle is a ruined tower house overlooking the Yarrow valley. It was unsuccessfully besieged by an English army in 1547, but was burnt the following year. In 1645 during the Civil War 100 royalist followers of the Marquis of Montrose were shot in the barmkin of Newark after the battle of Philiphaugh.

Newark Castle

C.M.Isherwood

On this walk you might come across men **burning the heather**. This is done on a rotational basis to provide nesting heather for the grouse and young shoots for the birds to feed on. Plumes of smoke tower up into the air and the fire that rages across a patch is kept well under control by the workers using beaters. Grouse shoots provide work and income for local people. Shooting begins on August 12th and continues until December 10th - but generally not every day.

1 Turn right out of the car park and walk past the fine house and on down the driveway to reach a triangle of grass. Turn left following a red waymark. Cross the estate road and continue down the waymarked track, known as the Lady's Walk, lined with lofty lime trees. Follow the track as it enters fine, mature deciduous woodland and continues west, high above the Yarrow Water. It then descends gently to the side of the hurrying water, which cascades, tumbles over rocks in its path and passes through deep pools. Look as you go for dippers, who enjoy the fast flowing water over rocks, then climb a row of easy steps to join a track and carry on. Cross the small stone bridge over the Newark Burn and a short way along, look up left to see ruined Newark Castle. Eventually you reach two cottages at Newarkmill. Wind round behind these and join the tarmac road that climbs quite steeply uphill and then bear right towards the ruin. It stands in a small area of grassland and is surrounded by young trees where you might like to take your first break.

2 Stroll on along the estate road. Soon after it winds right, look for the well-signed track, on the left, climbing into the forest and known as the Duchess's Drive. It climbs steadily for nearly a mile through Black Andrew Wood. The track is good and at first is lined with sitka spruce. Then there is younger sitka spruce over which towers elegant

116

Scots pine. Siskin, chaffinch, nuthatch, wren and great tit call from the trees. It is a long climb but nicely sheltered. Just after a pretty waterfall you reach a skewed junction of tracks where you take the way-marked higher one, which continues ahead. This is steeper but short and you can see light ahead. At the top go through the gate and out onto the extensive heather moorland.

3 Stride the good track as its climbs very gently, with ever improving views. The rolling moorland stretches away on both sides and it is a delight to be out on the tops after the confines of the forest. Look left to see, in the distance, the Eildon Hills and then go on the steadily climbing way. Just after passing through a gate, and before the track swings right at a waymark, turn left and walk a pleasing grassy trod, through the heather. At a split take the left track and as you near the top of Newark Hill, swing round left and then right to reach the summit and, sadly, its collapsed cairn. The view is superb.

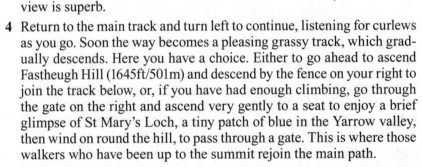

Scots Pine

Nuthatch

4 Return to the main track and turn left to continue, listening for curlews as you go. Soon the way becomes a pleasing grassy track, which gradually descends. Here you have a choice. Either to go ahead to ascend Fastheugh Hill (1645ft/501m) and descend by the fence on your right to join the track below, or, if you have had enough climbing, go through the gate on the right and ascend very gently to a seat to enjoy a brief glimpse of St Mary's Loch, a tiny patch of blue in the Yarrow valley, then wind on round the hill, to pass through a gate. This is where those walkers who have been up to the summit rejoin the main path.

5 Carry on the pleasing path as it winds right and goes on past a row of stone butts for concealing grouse shooters. Curve round with the track and continue your descent where you might see several grouse. Finally the track arrives at a gate into woodland. Go straight ahead through more fine mature deciduous woodland. Half way along the

track look for a pretty stone seat, encrusted in parts with moss. Look for a stone heart on its top part with the letters B & Q inscribed within; this represents the Buccleuch and Queensberry Estates and the dates added are 1864 and 1945. Continue down to the bottom of the track to join the tarmacked estate road where a few steps along you reach the car park.

Red Grouse

Practicals

Type of walk: *This pleasing walk starts off beside the lovely River Yarrow and continues to a ruined castle. It then follows the route of an old carriage drive, passing through woodland and over moorland.*

Total distance: 7 miles/11.3km

Time: 3–4 hours

Maps: OS Explorers 338 and 337/ Landranger 73

Walk 34

Broad Law

Park beside the cattle grid at the Megget Stone (space for 3 cars on the other side of the road from the gate), grid ref 151203. To get there take the minor road signed to Talla Fruid off the A701 at Tweedsmuir, or signed to Megget from Cappercleuch halfway along St. Mary's Loch. The stone and cattle grid are at the highest point on the road.

Broad Law is 2730ft/840m high and is the second highest hill in the Southern Uplands, after The Merrick in Galloway. It is a wide rounded hill with long spurs leading from it, and is grassy and relatively dry, giving very pleasant walking. The views from the top are excellent. It is somewhat disfigured on summit by an air traffic control installation and a telecommunications mast, but these are not apparent for most of the walk.

Megget Reservoir is the main source of drinking water for Edinburgh. The dam is the largest earth dam in Scotland. It took 6 years to build and was finished in 1983. It has a central concrete wall for reinforcement, then earth piled against it with a covering on the reservoir side of large stones. There are sundry access and service tunnels inside the dam.

1 Walk up the steep slope beside the fence to the top of the first summit, Fans Law 1916ft/582m. Bear right along the ridge where the slope slackens. The way can be boggy along here in wet weather. Look for masses of cloudberry in amongst the heather and bog cotton.

Megget Stone

2 Climb to the cairn on the next ridge, Cairn Law 2356ft/717m, and admire the view as an excuse for resting while you get your breath back. Do not bother with the next cairn, which would require climbing over a fence. Wind right below it to regain the ridge and again follow the fence up a gentle slope for 1¼ miles/2km over close-cropped turf to the summit of Broad Law. The summit cairn and OS trig point are at the fence corner, but the fence is quite low and easy to step over. Close to the summit is a strange edifice that looks like a helicopter landing pad surrounded by mushrooms. A notice on the door proclaims it to be the NATS Talla Navigation Aidair traffic control. It seems rather like an avian lighthouse. The view from here is superb in spite of the beacon and a telecommunications mast standing 660ft/200m away. You can see much of the Borders with the Eildon Hills prominent in the distance and the great whaleback of Cheviot. South are the hills leading up to White Coomb, and to the west the Lowther Hills and farther north Tinto and Culter Fell. If you have a clear day you can see Arran in the far distance.

3 The easiest way to return is to retrace your steps by the fence and if the weather closes in this is the safest thing to do. But on a good day bear left after about 1650ft/500m, diverging gradually from the fence as you descend onto an obvious spur to the left of the one you ascended. The walking is delightful over short grass. There is a small cairn at the edge of the spur, called Porridge Cairn 2497ft/768m, and you may see a raven which sometimes uses it as a perch. Carry on down; there is no path but the going is easy and you can see the ridge ahead. In spring and early summer, on this less frequented part of the fell, look for golden plover that nest here, and all year

1 km

1 mile

o Beacon
▲ Broad Law
↑③ 840m

N

Porridge
Cairn
759m.

Cairn Law
717m.
②

Wylies
Hill
609m.

④

Fans Law

Ⓟ

Megget Stone

Walk 34

Cotton Grass and Cloudberry

120

round for mountain hares. As you get lower a path appears which turns into a quad bike track. It runs down through the heather into a low col and then up the far side to the top of Wylies Hill. Bear slightly right from the top and go on along a ridge above the Megget Valley, with a good view of the reservoir to the left and St. Mary's Loch beyond it.

4   When you reach the end of this ridge, turn right to descend the steep slope into the valley, making use of the maze of sheep tracks that zigzag across the slope, and make the descent easier. Go down to the road and turn right. Walk along the verge, which in June and early July is carpeted with thyme, with green-veined white butterflies feeding on the plant. Curlews call in the distance, snipe drum, sandpipers fly over the burn and an oystercatcher stands sentinel by the bridge. Carry on up the road to the cattle grid where you left your car.

Golden Plover

Practicals

Type of walk: *Very pleasant. You reach the highest summit in the area, with the advantage of starting high. There is a clear path all the way up, running beside a fence, which forms a good 'handrail' to follow if the weather changes. On the way down there are not many paths but the walking is still easy. The descent from the end of Wylies Hill is steep but by making use of sheep tracks it is not too difficult.*

Total distance: 4½ miles/7.4km

Time: 4–5 hours

Maps: OS Explorer 336 and 330/Landranger 72

Walk 35

Loch of the Lowes, Pikestone Rig and Peniestone Knowe

Park at the junction of St Mary's Loch and the Loch of the Lowes, just beyond the fine statue of James Hogg, grid ref 238205. Access this from Moffat or from Selkirk.

James Hogg was born in the little cottage known as Ettrick Hall in 1771. From 1790–1800 he was shepherd at Blackhouse Tower and is often known as the Ettrick Shepherd. He was also a great poet and writer and a good friend of Sir Walter Scott.

Tibbie Shiels Inn was run by a widow, Isabella (Tibbie) Shiels, in the early 19th century. Sir Walter Scott and James Hogg used to drink here at the start or end of their walks. Today it also welcomes walkers. Look in the inn for the picture of Tibbie, if you have time for a visit. Near where you have parked, and also welcoming, is Glen Café, with a public toilet behind.

1   Leave the parking area and cross the bridge over the small burn that unites the two lochs. Take the first gate on the right to cross the

St Mary's Loch

sheep-nibbled turf, where oystercatchers probe the grass and fill the air with their piping. Cross the small bridge over the Crosscleuch Burn and continue along the loch shore on a narrow path. When well past the end of the plantation, on your left, climb a narrow path from the shore to a path higher up the slopes. If the loch is over full and the shore path impassable use the higher one. The latter leads to a gate at the end of the loch, the lower path reaches a wooden fence over which you will have to step.

2 Wind round right along the shore, following the waymarkers and then curve inland beside the burn on your right, climbing steadily to a gate and remaining well to the left of the Riskinhope Burn. Beyond the gate climb up the track to a waymark that directs you left and then right to a gate. Carry on along a green track and where it splits either go straight up or carry on along the zigzag – the two paths soon come together. Head on up the pleasing way as it climbs steadily into the hills, enjoying every step. As it begins to wind a little left you are confronted with two tracks. The right one, the one you really need has been used by the farmer and goes into a quagmire. Take the left one that climbs above the bog and then arc round, right, over drier ground, to pick up a dry tractor-marked path that soon joins the track you need.

3 Stride on up the track, with only one small section of mud to negotiate, to reach a Southern Upland Way (SUW) marker. Note this sheltered dell and then turn right to walk for nearly ½ mile/1km on a very good track climbing easily up the slopes of Peniestone Knowe, 1818ft/551m. As you go enjoy the superb views of the Tweedsmuir hills. When you reach the edge of the large summit plateau, the track ends. Ahead the area is full of boggy patches, tussocks of grass and lumpy bits of ground. You can see across all this to the actual summit, where three boundary fences meet and there is a small cairn, but getting there

presents a small problem. If you wish to get to the summit cairn pick your way carefully and return by the same route to the top end of the delightful track. As you return to the SUW the views down to the two lochs, nestling among the high hills, are spellbinding.

4 On reaching the SUW, turn right and almost immediately left to follow the waymarkers along Pikestone Rigg, a wide, grassy, level track. Follow the SUW as it winds right and descends steeply to Riskinhope Hope. Sadly the farm is a ruin. The valley is sheltered by large, overwhelming conifer plantations. Wind round, left, past a copse of pine and larch and then descend to cross a wooden footbridge over the Crosscleuch Burn to begin a steady climb to the corner of one of the plantations. Follow the SUW as it winds across a pasture, steadily moving away from the trees. Climb a stile and walk to a signpost. Stroll on through another clearing with plantations crowding almost all round.

5 Cross a burn in a gully on a long plank footbridge and go on to pass another signpost. Go over a cattle grid and begin your long descent on the reinforced track for nearly a mile to the valley below. Go past Tibbie Shiels Inn and over the bridge between the lochs to return to the parking area.

Oystercatchers

Practicals

Type of walk: *Most satisfactory. A splendid walk up into the hills, staying well up on generally good tracks, except for one very wet place which, mostly, can be avoided.*

Total distance: 7 miles/11.5km

Time: 4–5 hours

Maps: OS Explorer 330/Landranger 73 and 79

Walk 36

Drinkstone Hill and the Ogilvy Cairn and Seat

Park on the verge below the Ogilvy cairn and seat, grid ref 445188. Access is via the A7 between Hawick and Selkirk. Turn left on to a minor road at Ashkirk and follow it for about 4 miles/6.5km. The cairn is just over a mile beyond the bridge over the Ale Water, by Burnfoot.

The **Ogilvy Cairn and the Seat** are dedicated to W.H Ogilvy who was a well-known and much admired local writer and poet whose work perfectly captured the character of the area.

The **Borders Abbeys Way**, part of which is used on this walk, is a circular route taking in many of the main Border towns and four ruined abbeys, Kelso, Jedburgh, Melrose and Dryburgh. It is waymarked with an A superimposed on a W.

1 From the parking area descend, north, on a narrow path beside the road. At the wall, join the road, cross the cattle grid and go on down past a wood, on the right.

Continue on down round a bend in the road until you reach a gate on the right. Go through and climb uphill on a track beside the wall, with a deep ditch at first to the right. If it is very wet pick the driest way.

Ogilvie Cairn and Seat

125

Eventually the **Walk 36**
way improves
and comes to
a gate, which
you ignore,
into a splendid
planting of
deciduous trees.
Beyond wind right along
a sheep pasture, beside
the fenced plantation, to
go through a gate gap.
Stroll on uphill until you
can pass through a wooden gate in the fence, on the left. Turn left and
after a few steps, descend a grassy path through the trees to a little
valley below. Step over a stream and continue through an area with
notices saying that 'this is an area of historical interest', where you can
see evidence of a large deserted medieval settlement.

2 Follow the wide easy-to-walk-track, with the conifers planted well
   back, where you might spot a jay. Climb steadily to a heather-covered
   clearing. Here there was another settlement. Stroll on until you can
   turn left along a similar wide track through sitka spruce and larch,
   with banks of heather on either side. As you go listen for the songs of
   robins. Ignore a track off left and go on, winding right. Pass through
   another open area with a view of heather moorland. Then the way
   passes through larch, the haunt of siskins and crossbills. The track
   descends to a large clearing with sheep pasture to the left and then
   continues on beyond a junction. Here take a narrow path climbing
   right, with a sign for the Borders Abbeys Way and also for the Hawick
   Riding Route and begin a steady climb. Conifers again lie well back
   from the path and in any spaces are plantings of a variety of deciduous trees. The winding path rises and falls before descending again to
   a long valley where rows and rows of immature deciduous trees are
   thriving. Look for the large area of hawthorn bushes on the left. Cross
   a footbridge and continue up the other side and go on to pass through
   a gate out of the forest.

3 Ascend the huge field ahead to a gate on the skyline and continue on
   beside a fence on the right, to go through the next gate. Stroll, to the
   right, up beside the fence on the right towards a small block of conifers.
   Wind left before them, round the corner and head up to pass through
   another gate. Walk on a short way to stand beside the trig point on

Drinkstone Hill and enjoy the 360 degrees view of the many hills around. Then continue a short way along the fine grassy ridge. Down to your left is Drinkstone farm. On reaching a waymark with a blue arrow, directing you right, join a track coming up from the farm and walk right with it. The track soon becomes wide and muddy in parts, so pick the best way, keeping straight ahead and to the right of a small square of conifers and a few other trees, to a gate.

4 Beyond, walk ahead for a short way and then wind left on a poor sort of wide track, with heather moorland to the right and rough pasture to the left and with compensating fine views all around. Go through a gate and walk ahead on a better track. As you go look out for a narrow path dropping down right. This brings you to a wide grassy track. Look ahead to see in the distance a distinct path climbing up the slope ahead beyond a gate. Descend towards this. Then cross a shallow ford and start your climb up the track you could see earlier.

5 This soon fades but keep heading straight upwards on an indistinct way to pass through a gate, then walk straight ahead down a field to a gate in the valley. Climb up a good track, which curves a little, easing the gradient, and then at the top, turn right onto a reinforced track. Follow it as it winds back and forth. As it descends you pass a swampy pool away on the left and, to the far right, is Shielswood Loch with its boathouse. Continue on the rising track to reach the road, where, on a low hillock to the right, stand the cairn and the seat. Pause to enjoy the view and descend, right, down the hillock to the parking area.

Crossbill

Practicals

Type of walk: *This is an interesting walk that will be enjoyed by seasoned walkers who are good at map reading. The dry tracks through the forest are in considerable contrast to those over the higher moorland. Best not done after prolonged rainfall.*

Total distance: 8 miles/13km

Time: 4 hours

Maps: OS Explorer 331/Landranger 79

Walk 37

Rubers Law from Denholm

Park around Denholm's vast village green, grid ref 568186. Access to the village is by the A698 from Hawick or Kelso, or the B6358 from Jedburgh.

Denholm's unfenced village green is huge and well kept. A small section is given over to swings and roundabouts and there are a pair of goal posts. Houses surround the green, each one in keeping with all the others. Dominating the green and seeming to be a focal point for the charming village is the fine Leyden Monument. It was erected in 1861 to commemorate the life of Dr John Leyden who was born in Denholm in 1775. After qualifying he worked in India. He was also a poet and researched material for his friend Sir Walter Scott. On your walk around the village, look out for a thatched cottage where Leyden was born.

Rubers Law, 1392ft/424m, can be seen from many directions. The summit rocks are igneous, pushing through layers of Old Red

Rubers Law

Walk 37

Sandstone. This gives it a distinctive shape, with the top bounded by cliffs on all sides, except the north-east. The narrow cleft, 'Peden's Pulpit', on the summit, is named after Alexander Peden, a covenanter of the 17th century, who spent years living as an outlaw and preaching at illegal conventicles across southern Scotland. The Romans built a signal station here, and later tribes used the stones in their extensive fortifications.

1 Leave the Square by the A698, towards Kelso, following the sign for the Borders Abbeys Way, and walk along Main Street. Turn right up the Loaning with houses on both sides of the road. Then go on ahead, leaving the houses behind to walk a rough hedged track. At the top bear left at the T-junction, the way lined with bushes and young trees. Go with the track as it begins to wind right and look left to see a huge willow plantation. Pass through the kissing gate and carry on along the rough track with Scots pine to the right. In spring the trees resound to the songs of spring migrants.

2 Half way up towards a stile at the end of the plantation, turn right into the pines to walk a needle-strewn track which, indistinct at first, soon becomes wider and easy to follow. Stroll on the lovely way for ½ mile/1km until the path ends and ahead is a seemingly impenetrable sitka spruce plantation. Here walk left to follow a little path for a short distance to pass through a gap in a low wall. Pick your way ahead for a similar distance over pathless ground to join a distinct narrow path. Turn right and continue to the edge of the woodland. Go through a small gate into a field. A few steps ahead, take, on the left, a tiny stile and then go under the blue rubber tube, insulating the electric fence just beyond – it is easier to go under it than to climb over it.

129

3   Stroll on down the pasture, using a strip of raised grassland left by the farmer, when ploughing his field. Beside you continues the electrified fence and then the elderly wall with a fine plantation of Scots pine beyond. Pass through the next gate and go on down, walking the raised strip of grass. Follow it as it winds round a corner of the woodland and then on a short way to curve, right, beside a wall to go through a small gate. Then begin your climb up a huge field where you might spot several hares racing across the grass. To your right is a large pool, the haunt of heron and teal. Go on climbing to a gate, close to the plantation on your left, and walk ahead for a few steps. Bear right along a raised bank. Ignore the grassy track which soon starts its climb up the slope – this is to avoid a very wet patch - and go on a short way along before striking straight up left to join the distinct path, now quite dry. Continue on up, soon to come parallel with a ruined wall to your right, and walk on to the wall corner.

4   Ignore the clear track that goes off right, beside the wall, and walk ahead on an indistinct path, which soon becomes easy to follow. It leads into a glorious copse of Scots pine and very old larch trees and then goes on up the heather-clad slopes of Rubers Law. The path takes you easily upwards and passes through a delightful gully where more clumps of heather thrive. Ahead is the sheer north face of the Law. Wind round on a short curving path, right, and then, left, and stroll the lovely grassy sward round right again to reach the summit. The trig point stands out white at the highest point. The views are superb and you will want to try to name as many hills as possible, using your map. Here you may wish to wander a little, with care, to see remnants of the ramparts of an Iron-Age fort and to imagine what it must have been like when it was a Roman signal station. If you have youngsters with you warn them of the sheer drops from some of the delightful mini summits. Choose a sheltered corner here on the top for your picnic lunch.

Brown Hare

5   Retrace your steps all the way back to the little stile and the blue insulated electric fence. Beyond turn right to go through the gate, also taken earlier, and then a few steps

130

along, turn left on a narrow path through the deciduous woodland. Just after the path curves right by a wall, take a gate through it. Bear half left to descend steadily towards banks of gorse with fine woodland deeper in the valley. This path brings you down to a track. Turn left and carry on to the road where you turn right to walk a short way into Denholm.

Heron

Practicals

Type of walk: *This is a climb to a Law to enjoy. The first hedged path can be wet. The way through the wood is a joy. From then on it is mainly up but nothing too difficult.*

Total distance: 5 miles/8km

Time: 3–4 hours

Maps: OS Explorer 331/Landranger 80

Walk 38

Aithouse Burn and Wolfcleuchhead Waterfall, Craik Forest

Park in Craik Forest car park, grid ref 346082. Access this by taking the A7, south-west from Hawick.

Turn right onto the B711 to Roberton. Just beyond, take an unclassified road, signposted to Craik Forest and then more signs direct you, right, down to a delightful parking area. There is also a disabled car park and toilets here.

Craik forest is one of the largest areas of forestry in southern Scotland. Much of the planting was carried out in the 1960s and 1970s. This timber is now mature and in the process of being harvested. The information leaflet on the forest says that for every tree felled another two will be planted, many of them deciduous trees. The

Wolfcleuchhead Waterfall

forest provides timber for paper, furniture and the building industries. Many birds, otters, red squirrels and deer in the forest are shy creatures but are quite at home in Craik.

The **Wolfcleuchhead Waterfall** is on a tributary of the Aithouse Burn where the valley narrows and it is hidden until the last moment. It is a 26ft/8m fall of the apron type and most impressive after rain. Do not forget to take your camera.

There are several signed walks of varying length and several mountain bike trails. This walk to the waterfall on Wolfcleuchhead burn follows the **light blue markers.**

1 Follow the narrow path from the car park and walk on along the side of the Borthwick Water through larch, with a good view of large pastures and rolling hills beyond. Where the path ends, walk right up a grassy ride between conifers and bear left along a forest road. Turn right on a trod as directed by the waymark and at a split take a railed narrow path, right, and drop downhill as directed by the signpost, to come beside the pretty Aithouse Burn.

Walk 38

2 Walk left beside the chuckling burn below very tall trees, where siskins flit, with a clear-fell steep bank on the far side. Look underfoot for Norway spruce cones, well gnawed by squirrels, before climbing above the railed burn. Step over a little tributary and carry on close beside the water for a short way. Cross a small bridge and pass under more spruce. Go over another little bridge and stroll on, following the arrows, until you can cross the burn itself by a sturdy bridge to the opposite bank. Climb a little slope to a sign, directing you on to the waterfall and turn left.

3 Pass under a lofty stand of trees to cross a bridge over the burn again and wind left up a glorious gill, with the Wolfcleughhead Burn beside you. Here the trees have been clear-felled on the opposite bank,

133

allowing the sunlight to flood into the narrow valley. The burn now sparkles in the sun and the bank beside the path, in spring, is full of coltsfoot, celandines, primroses, barren strawberry, water avens and violets. Go past a picnic table and then wind round a corner and there ahead is the splendid waterfall, with a seat at its foot. Pause here for your break and perhaps take photographs of the plummeting water.

4 Return to the sign for the water-fall and climb the slope, left, to join the forest road. Walk right until you cross the road bridge over the Aithouse Burn and pass through an open barrier. Here look for a grassy path going off left, with the burn to your left. Go past a pool with seats beside it. Then the coniferous trees are left behind and over the rough pasture thrive a scattering of young deciduous trees. Just past an

Red Squirrel

old ruin, turn right on a narrower grassy path as it winds up through lofty larch. On reaching a sign for another waterfall, turn left to view, especially after rain when it is more impressive. Return to the sign and walk ahead to join another path where you turn right to the bird hide. Here you might spot robin, willow warbler, chiffchaff and red squirrels. Go back through the larch and on to join a reinforced path to reach several interesting plaques and the toilets. Turn right to walk ahead to pass the disabled car park and then the main parking area.

Practicals

Type of walk: *A lovely walk through the forest, with the Aithouse Burn for company, to visit a dramatic waterfall.*

Total distance: 3 miles/5km

Time: 1½ hours

Maps: Os Explorer 331/Landranger 79

Walk 39

The Waverley Line and Penchrise Pen

Park off the minor road to Barns Farm, grid ref 504096. To reach this drive south from Hawick on the B6399 for about 3 miles/5km and turn right once you have rounded the tight bend and before you have reached Woodford Bridge over the Slitrig Water. Drive up the unclassified road and pass under Barns Viaduct to a cattle grid. Just beyond it a track leaves the road on the left and there are grassy spaces here where you can park.

The Waverley Line was a double track railway line running through the Southern Uplands from Edinburgh to Carlisle. Built by the North British Railway Company the first part from Edinburgh to Hawick was opened in 1849 and the more complicated section from Hawick to Carlisle in 1862. Like the Settle and Carlisle Line it crossed difficult terrain with significant gradients and bleak moorland. There are several fine viaducts (two seen on this walk) and the long Whitrope Tunnel near the highest

Shankend Viaduct

point of the line (south of this walk). Against much public support the line was closed as one of Dr Beeching's cuts in January 1969. It was proposed earlier but was reprieved for two years. Now there are hopeful plans to reopen the line in 2014 from Edinburgh to Tweedbank, south of Galashiels.

1 The track divides almost immediately after leaving the minor road. Take the left fork which runs along above woodland and then swings right with a fence to the left. Go through a waymarked small gate by a field gate and continue down the next field to a gate in the bottom corner. Go through but do not venture onto the derelict bridge over the railway line to which the gate gives access; instead go through a wooden hurdle opposite onto the embankment and descend a fairly steep short path to the old trackbed.

Walk 39

2 Turn right along the delightful way, surrounded by trees and with primroses on the banks in spring. Listen for willow warbler and chiffchaff. Soon you can see Stobs Castle below you through a gap in the trees. The line runs along above the steep valley of the Slitrig Water, with spaces between the trees giving you lovely views. It is what a railway path ought to be like. It is wide (two track) and dry with nibbled grass grazed by sheep. There are field gates across in several places, usually with a small gate beside them, and often waymarked. Footbridges of sloping construction span the trackbed at intervals. Cross Primrose Wood and Penchrise Burn on high embankments, and

136

after 2 miles/3.5km you wind round a corner to see the fine Shankend Viaduct across the valley.

3 Here leave the old line at a waymark and go right on a track until it joins a larger track. Turn right here on a less obvious grassy track going up the hill. It soon divides, one branch keeping beside the wall and the other making a big loop, before coming together at the top of the hill. On your right is a large earthwork, the remains of an ancient settlement; you may like to take some time to explore it. In spring and summer curlews call and skylarks sing, and if you are lucky you may see black grouse. Head on to some derelict sheds, where the track suddenly becomes boggy. If you go round by the sheds the way is rather drier. Penchrise Pen now dominates the view in front. Carry on above a concrete retaining wall on a very rutted track; sometimes it is easier to walk on top of the wall. Then the track swings away from the wall and becomes easier, though damp and less distinct, as it runs across a slight rise to a gate. Go through and head downhill to where you can see the deeply rutted track starting again, and follow it into the valley where you cross the burn on an 'Irishman's bridge'.

Curlew

Black Grouse

4 The main track now swings right but take a left fork to a gate into a field. Beyond, cross a rather marshy area with a ditch and keep up by a ruined wall to a fence. Turn left and walk across the top of the field to a gate. Beyond the gate, walk uphill on a long diagonal, passing just below another fine settlement, which you might like to investigate. Then go on below a sheepfold to join a clear track contouring the hillside. Go through a gate and turn right off the track to climb beside the fence to a wooden hurdle. Negotiate this and then climb steeply up the slope to Penchrise Pen, 1428ft/439m, zigzagging over the short turf if necessary. There is a trig point on top and a magnificent wide view.

5 Descend by the obvious path on the western side of the hill, pausing to admire the earthworks below the summit; Penchrise Pen was a hillfort and part of another large settlement. Continue down the path to a gate into heather moorland and on down the narrow way past a small concrete shelter to join a sandy track by a waymark. Turn right and follow this track, with its wide extensive view over the Borders, for a mile, to a band of Scots pine on the right. Here take a grassy track which runs round to the right of the trees and up to Newton Hill, yet another splendid settlement, with two extensive banks and a ditch. Then carry on down the far side to regain the track. Follow this back downhill to your car.

Heather

Sparrowhawk

Practicals

Type of walk: *Delightful along the railway track and on the hill, although the moorland in between is very rutted and could be wet in bad weather. There are four extensive ancient settlements so there is much archaeological interest. The farmer keeps both sheep and cows on the land so make sure all gates are closed securely and do not take dogs.*

Total distance: 8 miles/13km

Time: 4–5 hours

Maps: OS Explorer 331/Landranger 79

Walk 40

Blackburn Falls from Newcastleton

Park in Douglas Square, Newcastleton, grid ref 482877. Access this by the A7 and then the B6357, signed Newcastleton and Canonbie, if coming from the direction of Carlisle, or the B6399 and B6357 from Hawick

Newcastleton, established in 1793, was a planned town designed by William Keir of Whithaugh for the 3rd Duke of Buccleuch who wished to settle handloom weavers. It was built on a grid pattern with lots of space and a large open area for people to gather, called Douglas Square. Sadly the handloom business was not a success mainly because of the remoteness of the village. So to help the inhabitants thrive, each household was given some land, 1 acre for single storey houses and 2 acres for those with two storeys. Many people grew crops and kept animals for food.

Blackburn Falls

1 Leave the square at Newcastleton by the south-west corner to walk along Langholm Road. Where it makes a sharp turn left go ahead up steps into deciduous woodland. Turn right and carry on with a fence to the right, with trees beyond. Soon, cross the stile over the fence and descend to a bridge over a narrow gill to climb steps up the banking and then carry on up the gill on the winding track through the glorious woodland. Tracks and boardwalks then take you down along the other side of the gill. Continue on and look for tree-creeper, woodpecker and crossbill. As you stroll through this lovely woodland, make sure you follow all the little wooden bridges and boardwalks because they do take you clean-shod over muddy patches and ditches.

Walk 40

2 At the end of the woodland, leave by a stile and bear left up a wide track and climb steadily up the edge of Pathhead Moss. The way is generally dry but can be muddy where the tractor has been along to feed the white cattle. Pass through a gate and follow the wide grassy trod that drops down and then up a little towards Blackburn farm. Join the access track to the farm and turn right along it. Wind right with the track to pass between a fine barn and the farmhouse. Beyond the gate, wind downhill to reach the wooden footbridge across the Black Burn. Beyond, at the junction of paths, turn left and stride a wide track, through fields, easy to walk but which also maybe used by vehicles. This keeps parallel with the pretty Black Burn, where grey wagtails cavort and you might spot a dipper.

3 Follow the track as it begins to veer away from the burn and then begin a steady climb through long swathes of rough moorland as the track bears right. Eventually you reach a Y-junction, where you take the left turn and descend to Hog Gill. Cross the ford on flat stones or, if in spate, on large boulders. Turn left and wind round with the track as it climbs out of the gill. Go on to pass a fine round stone sheep pen, and continue climbing more gently to a gate across the track, which slopes steeply down beyond. At this point turn left along a rather wet path, signed to the Blackburn Falls. Soon the path, dry now, carries on

along the edge of a very deep gill. Walk with care and look down to see part of the Falls as you progress towards the 'nose' of the grassy cliff. A little path winds down the ravine for a short way and this gives you a much better view – but only attempt this if you know you are able to climb back up. It is not a descent for those who have no head for heights.

4 Return by the same route, along the wet path to the track, where you bear right and continue all the way to the wooden bridge where you walked sharp left. Here turn left away from the bridge and stroll over to a gate in the wall. Beyond, walk left and follow a grassy track, which climbs steadily. Stay with it as it winds round right and then right again to pass between a cottage and a barn. Continue a short way to a gate and then a few more steps to another on the left. Drop down a large pasture to go through a gate in the bottom right corner. Carry on left on a wide track through more rough moorland, which soon improves as it comes close to Ralton Burn far down in its deep wooded gill. Wind round Raltonside and continue on down the track to reach the access track to Roan farm.

5 Turn right and walk on almost to the road to go, right, onto the disused railway track, now a delightful way edged with pleasing deciduous woodland, with the road to your left. Watch out for where you need to join the road to cross the bridge over the Black Burn. Continue on the road, past two bungalows, and then drop, left, down signed steps into a large field beside the lively Liddel Water. Dawdle on until you can take, right, the second paved road, which will bring you back to the square.

Treecreeper

Practicals

Type of walk: *Delightful countryside and rough moorland, a great contrast. A dramatic waterfall in a very steep-sided gill. Pleasing return almost all downhill.*

Total distance: 7 miles/11.4km
Time: 3–4 hours
Maps: OS explorer 324/Landranger 79

Walking Scotland Series
from Clan Books

MARY WELSH has already compiled walkers' guides to each of the areas listed: material for guides covering the remaining parts of Scotland is being gathered for publication in future volumes.

Titles published so far:

1. WALKING THE ISLE OF ARRAN
2. WALKING THE ISLE OF SKYE
3. WALKING WESTER ROSS
4. WALKING PERTHSHIRE
5. WALKING THE WESTERN ISLES
6. WALKING ORKNEY
7. WALKING SHETLAND
8. WALKING THE ISLES OF ISLAY, JURA AND COLONSAY
9. WALKING GLENFINNAN: THE ROAD TO THE ISLES
10. WALKING THE ISLES OF MULL, IONA, COLL AND TIREE
11. WALKING DUMFRIES AND GALLOWAY
12. WALKING ARGYLL AND BUTE
13. WALKING DEESIDE, DONSIDE AND ANGUS
14. WALKING THE TROSSACHS, LOCH LOMONDSIDE AND THE CAMPSIE FELLS
15. WALKING GLENCOE, LOCHABER AND THE GREAT GLEN
16. WALKING STRATHSPEY, MORAY, BANFF AND BUCHAN
17. WALKING AROUND LOCH NESS, THE BLACK ISLE AND EASTER ROSS
18. WALKING CAITHNESS AND SUTHERLAND
19. WALKING THE SCOTTISH BORDERS AND EAST LOTHIAN

Books in this series can be ordered through booksellers anywhere.
In the event of difficulty write to
Clan Books, The Cross, DOUNE, FK16 6BE, Scotland.

For more details, visit the Clan Books website at
www.walkingscotlandseries.co.uk